Getting A Miracle

Light Covering Darkness

To Jona
long time friend

By D. J. Shrewsbury

D. J. Shrewsbury

WHY I WROTE THIS BOOK

Hi all: It seems like when we are having difficult times with great needs, times of family troubles or just plain sickness and pain, it is time to go to God with great gusto and fervent prayers. These are the times it seems that poetry comes to me with its truest meaning. For when we are in our greatest needs and the most difficult times of our life then we are more apt to reach out beyond what we are. I am one who has endured great pain, lost love, and just sitting at deaths door, yet needing to stay to raise my boys as they only had me. In my searching I have found God to be real in my life and through much praying have become a miracle receiving strong believer.

I am in hopes that non-believers as well as believers alike can find some goodness in my writings. I do not want to offend anyone and believe that God loves all mankind. I have found the Way, becoming a believer in Jesus Christ and believe He will finish the good work that He is has started in me. I have hope in my heart that all mankind will find his or her way into heaven. Maybe if you try to see where my heart has been in getting my Miracle, in my prayers, and how God has lead me to this physical healing it may help you as well. That we all might come to know the power of His resurrection, the freedom in His Grace, in the fullness of God.

These writings come from many years of studying the Word, long hours, days and years of praying and being open to the Spirit of God. They come through many people that God has put before me through my life and the teaching God has granted through their love and obedience to Him. May He use these poems and writings for His Glory. I hope and pray that I have not gone off from His Word in them. May He bless and be with you all.   IN HIS GRACE DJS

PRAYER FOR ALL

Father, I pray that You would hear my prayer and thank You Lord that You have given Love to man. Your Word states that You first gave Love to us. Lord, I pray that You would fill me with Your Love that my heart would be like Yours. Help me to love my brothers and sisters with Your kind of Love. Lord, let me see the world through Your eyes that I can make a good judgment of the action of others and myself. Let me know the difference between my thoughts and Yours.

Lord I have come to know that scripture is all true, that Jesus is Your Son and He has opened a door that we may come to You. Scripture states that we can come boldly to the Throne Room of God with our prayers. You will indeed listen and help us in our hour of need. I do realize that You are God and that all things that I may think as cruel such as hatred, starvation, wars, and just the way man treats each other through selfishness and pride are not from You. I have learned there is a devil and he does have power when man allows him. Satan has much hatred of man when man chooses Gods ways over his. He will then offer man as he did Jesus in the desert earthly things in hopes he will decide to live in the world and its ways. Lord help to keep him away as I submit to You.

I do know that my prayers and my slowly changing to Your image by Holy Spirit direction, through Your power and Your leading I do receive Your Love and strength. I know that many times You have intervened in my life and saved me from death of the physical and the spiritual by Your Love. I have finally learned that You can be trusted, to not judge You in the horrors of the world but to thank You for Your Love and kindness. I see the beauty of the earth in a new way in my new life. You have given salvation, and because of this I see everything in a different way, a way that gives life and beauty instead of death and ugliness.

I understand that You have a plan and it will be completed on earth and most likely in my life. I know You finish every work You take on and that You will complete the things in my life that are best for the people I meet and love, and myself. In my hardest moments I know You are there and will not let anything occur that You think will not help me. Now Lord I pray that You would finish the good work You have started in me and that You will give the desires of my heart that are for good and according to Your Word. I know the work of God is to believe in Jesus and I do. Now Lord direct and guide me and make my path clear before me. Show me the things You would like me to do here in the days that I live. Lord let Your Spirit become strong in me. Help me not to judge but let You, help me to forgive as You forgive me, and help me to be more like You.

We all need more of You. Let the world see that You are not just a possibility but as God the creator of Heaven and Earth the Father of Jesus, and all of mankind. I look forward to Your return and hope You have much mercy for man. I love You, Come Lord!

TABLE OF CONTENTS

TITLE POEMS

Getting a Miracle

Hold on to your faith
Our Lord is very near
Hold on to your faith
Turn away from fear
Hold on to your faith
He measured it to you
Hold on to your faith
He wants you to be true
Believe in your healing
Constantly pray
Speak to your problem
He'll take it away
Believe in our God
Believe you are healed
You must believe God
A Physician so skilled
Pray on your knees
Pray on your face
Find a friend in Jesus
Run the good race

Light Covering Darkness

When the lights are turning low and all is so dim
Darkness begins to settle the lamp wick to trim
With the lamp turning down ready to set to sleep
Resting for a while on the horizon the sun does peep

My darkness was in illness taking from me my life
Disease a dark hold on my body cutting as a knife
I prayed, I cried, I prayed my life fading away
Doctors said it was over, darkness in the day

Still needed on this earth, children relying on me
Deeper into His Spirit, my prayers on my knees
Body getting weaker now before God on my face
Believing, desiring a miracle this is no disgrace

Walking and talking with God all the day through
Pleading for a miracle, He could do it, this I knew
Transplant list, weaker, the light was growing dim
Most thought within my mind and spirit now to Him

Sitting in Specialist office, he said I would surely die
I said Jesus heals, I would live, I looked him in the eye
His Spirit fell upon me I told everyone around
Jesus is the answer and He would not let me down

That Light continues to shine, His lamp is on high
Like the bright morning sun comes up into the sky
Now seven years later, my life is in His hand
Light covering darkness, like footsteps in the sand

AUTHOR AND WIFE POEMS

Our Journey Together In You

I have chosen a bride, she has accepted me
She has chosen a groom, I accepted her
We have our rings and so much more
In our love, with the eagles we shall soar

Special is she in all her ways
Equally yoked, joy in our praise
To worship the Lord, together we do
A real relationship, in God so true

With each other we have the same
For our love will always be in Jesus name
His blessing has touched our hearts you see
Our marriage in Him will be all it can be

Now to lift up God, to praise His name
Thanking Him, His word we claim
He is our all in all, our life, our plan
So very blessed is this woman and man

This is the wedding poem I wrote for my
Wife

My Girl

Christian Café a new dating site, met a girl
It probably won't work, should I give it a whirl
Should I take a chance, is she thinking the same
She probably is actually just playing a game

She wants to meet, with a friend she will be
She'll be dressed in sweater I will surly see
Doesn't trust to be alone, neither do I
Should I look to find her, should I leave or try

Why should I meet her, it always turns bad
Also know it will probably turn out sad
Am I building this up bigger than life
Guess I just hope maybe I'll find a wife

I gave it the try and took the big chance
Hugged each other and did a new dance
I married this girl and I'm happy you see
She is more than I thought she'd ever be

Now we're married with our first anniversary
All started because Jesus died on that tree
For we believe in our Savior evenly yoked
We laugh and we love and enjoy a good joke

GROWING IN GOD POETRY

Ageless

When I was a small boy of five years old
I did basically what I was told
I wanted to be older, maybe ten or so
Then into life I could really go

Then I was ten and wanted to be a teen
For all the teens just seemed so keen
Keen wasn't it, still wanted older to get
I would be twenty-one in just a little bit

Drinking age, adulthood wasn't what I thought
Now I looked to marriage and family a whole lot
Married now she and I, my life was now great
Start a family, have children, I just couldn't wait

Had a child, and then there were three around
Took in others, growing family, I felt sound
Then one day my wife just up and went away
Found another, thought she would now play

Broken family, if I could again be ten
I'd do better if I could just do it again
Marriage again but it was to no avail
More children now to tell the tell

Loved them dearly but the union went down
Calling to God with face on the ground
Brought them up the best that I could
Did everything that I knew I should

Now I look back one more time again
Oh my gosh not back to ten
I think not, I'll just go on now
Spirit of God will show me how

Always In Joy

In the midst of trial and tribulation
I find myself with a smile so wide
Feeling Your presence I do not run
For I know You Lord are on my side

If you are having a day that's so hard
And you know there is no way to win
Just rest in His peace for he will guard
Leaps and bounds away from all sin

Just start to sing and praise His Holy name
Let go and let God, trusting in Him alone
Live this way; you'll never to be the same
Your victory will soon be set in stone

Then you may know that He's in control
Begin to walk out of this hardship as well
It's not by your work but by His Godly role
Your story will turn out good you will tell

As baptism is under the water, coming up anew
In Jesus death many miracles from the cross
We must die to ourselves, His sacrifice is true
Do not be worried about our change or loss
He paid the cost

Another Miracle

It seems this is my regular call these days of life
To need Your presence to prove You Lord, in truth
For it is only You Lord God that can truly please us
Father, I need another miracle in the name of Jesus

Holy Spirit my words are inspired to who You send
For it is only You that can bring another to Jesus
I have some close to me that don't see You as true
Holy Spirit saturate me when I speak of You

There is no other way for us to reason it through
For there is much in the world, to say You are false
I know You Lord and my family needs the same
You must be God in Spirit as we share, Your name

My position in life has become real in Your care
Many a man teaches You are not much to believe in
Those around me I can share with, they won't bow
Oh for them to know, Lord please show them how

Direct and guide me so I can speak of Your life
That it didn't end on the cross, as many believe
So fill me Jesus with Holy Spirit, the Word true
So love ones can be saved both Gentile and Jew

Please help me to bring my love ones to You soon
Speak to them each that they may truly know for real
I pray to You Lord Jesus, You are the only way I know
That You Jesus are God and in You they may grow

On Calvary salvation is what I saw
Oh God my Spirit grieves for my children all
Let them Holy Spirit now hear Your call
Speak now to my children, one and all

Everyday

Be In My Dreams Lord

When life has been hard all day long
Seems like everything has gone wrong
Your presence is distant or so it seems
Hard to even see my hopes and dreams
I love You Lord

When all that I try seems hard without reason
Seems like I'm living in the wrong season
Calling on Jesus but hearing not a word
Where are You Lord , has anyone heard
I Love You Lord

Needing You so much, feeling quite alone
Is it me being distant, am I in the wrong zone
Why can't I see You in my heart or my mind
Why can't You come to me, it would be so kind
I Love You Lord

I know You Love me, I believe this to be true
Because You first Loved me that I can Love You
Waiting now, sadness in heart, tears in eyes
Will You come to me, going to sleep with a sigh
I Love You Lord

Fun & True

It's so fun to laugh and just enjoy each others humor
To give a hug, do a belly laugh, to sit without rumor
To share a good thing that has happened in your life
To a good friend, even better if it is your wife

Driving a car or motorcycle makes us happy as can be
Its fun driving around and looking at what we see
Lovely when your son or daughter makes you proud,
big smile
When you are healthy and do realize it, just run a mile

To cook a great meal, having friends and family to enjoy
Bringing home a new song to dance with your girl or boy
A flower for your love one brings a big smile to her face
Remember to enjoy your life, better to slow down the pace

If you are racing to and fro in the fast lane as well
You will not have very much of a story to tell
Then when you get home everyones waiting on you
They will joyfully be happy for daddy's home too

So slow down the pace, see the beauty before you
Watch the leaves move, as the wind passes through
Look into the eyes of all those who you love now
They are the very best you will ever show how

To be happy and to live in the Love God gave you
That they also will be smiling and happy as you too
For not what you say but what they see you do
Will be what they become, so do what you do, true

God

He is everywhere you may look they say
Right beside you walking through the day
He watches and hears as you work and play
His Spirit is with you as you go to bed and pray

He can help you as you face the problems of life
He will answer the prayers of a husband and wife
In your darkest hour, He can take away the strife
He cuts deep in your thoughts like a two edged knife

He's right there with you when you wish He were gone
His Holy Spirit is here to help you to turn from wrong
Turning the banging in your head into a sweet song
You'll be longing for His presence the whole daylong

He sent His Son Jesus to make a way back to Him
So that for many of the world it won't be so dim
Earth is terrible, when trouble fills its cup to the rim
Wow, to watch Him remove it, like pruning a limb

After Jesus came back home sacrifice in hand
He sent His Holy Spirit in His place to man
Forgiveness of sin what a lovely, beautiful plan
By the power of this action every man can stand

In the presence of God, His Son, and Holy Spirit too
And all your loved ones that found the message to be true
So the least we can do when our family and friends are blue
Share the life of Christ with them and their creation
will be new

God is One

God the One is and was before the world began
Seeing that man was alone He created him a companion
He was and is Spirit yet created His image in man
They together numbered many a child as a beach, its sand

One God was three before the world was created by word
The earth was formed into land, water,
and beauty you've heard
His word became as substance by His faith
and power as He can
All the birds of the air, creatures of the sea,
trees and such began

The Father, Holy Spirit and Jesus, Trinity are One
His Son became physical, born of a virgin,
half Spirit He's One
Holy Spirit bringing His seed to become
the life of the womb
His plan for Salvation of all mankind would
begin in a tomb

He gave up the ghost, sacrificed Himself, freed us from sin
The gift is free to receive, for the price was paid
in full by Him
His resurrection power, who believes in His Son
shall never die
Devil was surprised to see Gods plan complete,
Son died, Father cried

A gift the creator did give on a cross-covered
with blood and purity
That the sins of man could be washed away
that he could live eternally
Thanking You Jesus, One of the three that gave
eternal life to me
As all gave and still give, Their plan of Oneness includes
all family

That as the Son was One with the Father
and Holy Spirit and they with Him
That we are One in Him, His Spirit residing in us
fills our cup to the brim
That we are brother, friend, companion,
and look to our Savior in Jesus
In His plan He always wanted us to conform
to and let Him please us

Thank You Father God, Holy Spirit, and thank You Jesus
We are in You also we believe, a true relationship calls us
For You are Holy, Holy, Holy, You are always One
So again, say I thank You Father, Holy Spirit, and Son

Heavenly Bound

High above earth in the skies I now soar
On the wings of eagles through celestial doors
Spirit around, above and below
Face of God I pray that now You will show

Not to blind or absorbed me, here I stand
But to indwell me and love me as only You can
Dressed in white, clean, pure and Holy are You
Presenting my body, sacrificing my humanity too

Suffering is real; Jesus did, some for us as well
Would rather not endure the pain, would rather not tell
Sincerely say I that we must all suffer and cry
Sorely I say there is a time for us to die

Written down clearly as You open the book of life
Wavered not from the hope, moved not by the strife
Jesus I do follow from the hope in salvation
Spoken of eternal are You from the creation

Rising now, heavenly bliss all about me
Forever not seen except from that cross and tree
In death I still follow, heaven now in my sight
Good bye cruel world, Jesus, oh my the light

Home Groups

Thank You Lord, lift us up
To the upper room we go
Praying Holy Ghost open the gate
Tongues of fire shall saturate

Giving ourselves up, His plan
All over the earth, we stand
In His Spirit we truly know
For the fire continues to grow

Praying in Spirit and truth
From Father through Jesus the proof
Holy Spirit now moving about
Sincere trust and Love no doubt

Submerged in His Spirit, His peace
His love, His grace, His release
Given our Faith, a measure
His anointing, oh the treasure

Lets climb those stairs
Each step our Prayers
The upper room above
Spirit, gentle as the dove

The finger of God will appear
Our joy so full, He's near
Our cup is overflowing
His Spirit ever growing

Lifting His name
Flames of fire came
Miracles for you and me
Let us be True, Believe

Homeless-Human

Entertaining thoughts of failure and despair
Done all I can do and pray and pray for His care
Feels like I'm losing ground as I trudge onward
Have you experienced the same, or have you heard

One can become homeless by choice or some great loss
Most don't realize the hardship, suffering, and the cost
Once one is down so hard to climb back up
No shower, no bed, at home the kids,
no milk in the cup

Leaving behind your love ones, not bringing them along
You might find a way, searching the city,
no laughter or song
For God must help but am I worthy enough
to ask for a hand
Could I with His help take a strong and decisive stand

Guess life is not fair for one is rich and one is so poor
One lives on the street, fights the fight, has no door
To the rich his needs are met he thinks little of the other
Have you ever driven down a street and seen one,
your brother

For we all come from One God, He created us all
The rich, the poor, gifted, educated, short and the tall
So next time you drive by don't classify them all the same
For some of them are truly out of luck and are not to blame

Homeless Man

A homeless man lying in a box nearby
Empty bottle of wine so close at his side
Deeply sleeping, peoples' feet scurry by
No one knows he's in there or why

Earlier, two months gone by fast
To take a look into this mans past
We see him with love ones near
Family time, children and wife so dear

Then on that eventful dark night
More sadness happened than is right
A knock on the door and a gun, oh no
Turned around, said for them to run, go

Everything turning dark, I've been hit
From this moment on he remembered not a bit
In the hospital he woke, friends, tears in their eyes
Where's my family he asks and begins to cry

That night brought murder took all he had loved dear
They were all now gone; my God, tear after tear
What happened, I can't seem to bear the truth
He put on his clothes, for now nothing could sooth

He ran to the streets never to look back again
His life was now gone, all he loved and had been
Now lying in this box he wished he would die
The shock took his reason, how could he try

A light descending on the box, he opens his eyes
They're carrying him out, his body, last sighs
They're taking me away, who is holding my hand
I'm Jesus, come your family waits in the new land

Jesus Said Move Mountains

Jesus said to His disciples and us too
With faith we can move mountains, true
Just the faith of a mustard seed so small
Can make that tree grow strong and tall

Said if we ask, seek, or knock and trust
More of the Holy Spirit will be with us
If we believe it to be done without doubt
Expecting a miracle we begin to shout

We walk in His Spirit and let Him lead
Living a life worthy, asking of our need
At cliffs edge holding on, all that we are
His presence is with us; He'll never be far

What am I sharing as I write in verse
We don't have to live under the curse
Can walk with Him all the days of our life
In hardship and pain, loving family and wife

I wish I could tell of the suffering in my days
We must suffer some, as He molds His clay
Outcome is great, overcoming all that we face
Living in Love, Joy and Grace, the human race

Open Your Eyes

Look at the world; tell me what do you see
Wars and hate in the religious community
Destroying the life God has given, another
Can't do it, and the same time call him brother

Everyone thinks he has found the right way
People have thought this way forever a day
Need I say more, can you see it for yourself
What stands in your way, the need for wealth

Is it that you like another to look up to you
Do you think it right everything you do
Can you admit a mistake, can you change
Sometimes things just need to be rearranged

What are your priorities are they from His Grace
Do you truly know your life is in the right place
Fall on your knees take another look at the people
Looking up now I can see they are Gods steeple

We are the Church do we live like we are one
We look into each others eyes do we see the Son
Take a moment and another look from your heart
All are children of God; let us all make a new start

Peace Of God

Jesus said He would leave us His peace
The peace beyond understanding
Even though tribulations will not cease
Living in Him will give us a soft landing

Life on earth is very hard at times, living
Feelings and loses will emotionally hurt
Peace from the Father to us He is giving
Life in Him we will share a coat or a shirt

All about Oneness with God and mankind
As Jesus overcame the world and its ways
We too have this peace when we are in a bind
Let the Peace of God rule our hearts all of our days

It surpasses understanding, guarding mind and heart
Being at peace with those who work for loves sake
Now Jesus is the King of Peace from the very start
In His Spirit trusting Him alone our peace we do make

Let us work for God in unity of Spirit, bonding in peace
With faith, hope, love, in Oneness running a good race
Praying always for His presence to saturate and release
His Spirit will guide us, to the fullness of His Grace

Prayerfully Asking

Father You said to ask, seek, and knock
Seek Him for His presence, not by the clock
Ask You Father in Your Son Jesus name
Find Him we will, never be the same

When we ask for His help, a miracle touch
Might be in health, hardship, sorrow and such
We need His Spirit to assist us, His presence
Nothing too big for Holy Spirit, makes sense

In our seeking we shall have more of His Spirit
High in Spiritual places we pray and He hears it
With more of His Spirit our words become strong
Problems begin to take on the appearance of gone

Co-heirs with Jesus what a calling we have so true
Hard to believe, He is our Savior and friend too
To be like Him when we see Him, the glory they're of
Fitting into His Spirit, like a well fitting glove

Seeking first the kingdom of God, His righteousness
Pick up my cross and follow Him, no stress
My needs being met as I pray by day and night
Asking by the Word I know I'm doing it right

Read The Word Daily

May I give advice to all that do read
Reading the Bible will give you a seed
It will plant in you the truth of mankind
Answers become clear like reading a sign

If you believe in God and Jesus is His Son
Then to read the Bible should be a little fun
For all through its pages is about your life
Your friends and your children and your wife

If you are single there is a lot for you
Divorced man or woman in this book too
Have a problem that keeps you from the Lord
Read the Word it will show ways to cut the cord

If you just need a friend, there is none better
He will be by your side in good and bad weather
Salvation is clear to those who want to be His
Will clear your mind, if too filled with that biz

If you think an old dog can't be taught new tricks
Just read some proverbs you'll have some kicks
Then if you are ready to accept Jesus, do it right now
Hey, will all go to heaven with Him and do it in style

Saving Our Nation

One nation under God are we
Our trust brought safety you see
In God we trust, this we did say
Are we going to change this today

God has always loved mankind
He has taken many out of a bind
But always when we turn away
He stops helping, we need Him to stay

By our choice we could lose it all
No longer hear His beckon and call
No longer have His protection you see
Are you willing to sacrifice, your family

Our nation is strong, or so it may seem
Yet in Him we live and have our being
We could be lost like many before
If we push Him away and close the door

Now listen close and listen clear
We need our Lord and need Him near
He will forgive if we are on bended knee
If we live for Him, you and me

Seeking You still

Singing to You the praise is real
When the singing stops I'm seeking You still
Never enough desiring You more
On bended knee, face to the floor

You're so close yet so far away
So I seek You more each and every day
Longing to have Your presence, so real
Spirit You sent, yet seeking You still

When am I fulfilled, will it be today
When will I feel you are here to stay
Guess it will be when You roll back the skies
Then on that day I'll see in Your eyes

Can we have that relationship now
Will You show me the way and the how
Will You walk me down the road
For You live in me, this I am told

So show me how to live within You
Gently show me how to be true
Meet my needs, humble I am
Give to me my own Godly plan

Stay Put

Find a church where you are comfortable
Don't try to find an error in the message
If you are looking for error you will find
Try not to be the preacher or look for a sign

Be a peacemaker and true to Gods Word
Judge not and forgive we all make mistakes
Submit to God and worship the Lord
Love one another; it'll sharpen your sword

To love God is easy this I will say
Love Him with your whole heart and mind
Your strength too, and your neighbor as well
When you do this love will swell

Just stay put when you find your place
And if you leave it is no disgrace
Just walk the walk that you do talk
Fly in His Spirit, float like the hawk

To worship Jesus is a personal thing
Just come in and your family do bring
Sing to the Lord with heartfelt song
Doing this I say you can't go wrong

Take Me To Calvary

Take me back to Calvary
Take me to the place you died for me
Into the darkness, the sting of death
Took my sins and bowed Your head

God of the universe, controlling all
Could have required anything at His call
Yet by free will He gave his life
To choose You to give a new life

What great love to give Your life
Then to call us His bride, His wife
A perfect walk too hard for us
You sent you son, our Lord Jesus

He told us, showed us, how to live
Then He gave us all He could give
Made a way to heaven for man
Opened the door as only He can

Resurrection power to heaven He went
Holy Spirit to earth He sent
To care for each and every need
And all there is to do is just believe

Now back to the message at hand
He died on the cross, being His plan
To save us all from the torture of hell
Releasing the prisoners from Satans jail

Taking from the devil, the keys of death
Giving His Love, His heart, His breath
Just reach your hand out to Him
As He takes it, He takes your sin

Now live a life worthy and true
Do all you can possibly do
For He gave all He could give
So that you and I can really live

The Way

Paul said to imitate him as he imitated Christ
Jesus said if you see Him you see the Father
Said He is the way the truth and the light
Let us keep the ways of Jesus in our sight

Early disciples church was called the way
The way of righteousness the way of salvation
They were moved by the leading of the Holy Spirit
When they spoke and prayed the people would hear it

Jesus said He must leave so the Holy Spirit would come
Said the Holy Spirit would guide us into the truth, Him
That believing in the works He did, we would also do
Even greater things we will do, asking of Him true

So what am I saying and do want you to hear
Jesus is alive, in His Spirit He gives gifts
That no one can say that Jesus is the Lord
Except he do it by the Holy Spirits cord

In His Spirit we have relationship with Him
In His Spirit we will find His Presence true
It is up to us and our free will to follow close
I want my relationship with Him to be the most

So sing and praise in His Spirit with heart full
Presence falling upon us, like a gentle white dove
To live in His Spirit, to walk in the Light bright
Will bring our Father and Jesus into our sight

Walk The Walk

You have heard it said to walk the walk
Not to be different in your walk from your talk
Don't be alarmed, not trying to offend you
Just that we can enjoy so much more if we do

When we are wishy washy, not being our best
Are we thinking that on earth this is all a test
Let us be truthful and see what we see
Let us love one another, speaking of you and me

For if we say that we are truly the church
Two or more together sitting on our perch
Let the Lord be with us and life be His Word
Not the words that from this earth we have heard

To know Jesus is to conform to His image and ways
For a man who loves Him, in His ways he stays
Doesn't stray to far without repenting to Him
For if a man does, his light begins to dim

Then darkness becomes normal his lamp is out
Sharing not a word for he's lost his true route
Come back my friend and do better this time
Let the creation be poetic and let it rhyme

So, talk the talk and walk the walk this day forth
Like a compass needle goes to true north
Be steadfast and true grow daily in the Lord
And when the devil comes just pull out your sword

We Can't Trick God

We live a life with a forked tongue, you know it
Fresh and salty coming from the same mouth
Now we know this is not what God expects from us
Like a compass with true north being south

Can we change our ways the bible says we can
We can repent; go the other way on this day
The provision is there, take heed and stand
Or in this confused state do we choose to stay

Some of us need to come together and band
Not be deceived by every word that we hear
We choose to do wrong when right is in sight
Some know the way and know it so clear

So if this is you, or if it is I, or another one we see
Take on your own part with Father-God that you love
Pray more Holy Spirit to show you the way
If you ask Him to join with you, you'll fit like a glove

Now listen to His voice still soft in your ear
Take time to know Him and the direction He sets
Live now your best for Jesus did it for you
When the devil wants your soul, he cannot get

Now love one another a new commandant was given
From the Lord Jesus speaking clearly to all man
So come out of yourself, share the gifts that you have
Don't think you can't for I do know you can

MORE OF YOU LORD JESUS
AND PRAISE-FELLOWSHIP

He Gave His best

Good night Lord, I'll see You in my dreams
No awareness in the night, or so it seems
Trust You my Lord to see me through
Knowing for sure, I'm sticking with You

Good morning Father, had a nice sleep, thank You
Heard a breeze in the trees outside my window too
Peace fell upon me like the sandman touch
The birds are now chirping, singing, and such

Now thankful this morning for life goes on
Darkness brightens by the rising of the sun
In Your Love, I have all the hope that I need
Our Lord, Holy Spirit I will listen and take heed

Glad I came into Your Life, now part of the One
Received by Your most cherished, Your very own Son
Jesus my friend, earths best we do have
What a wonderful Life Lord, You gave us love

The gift You gave, I won't take it lightly
I believe in Your promises not just barely or slightly
I don't want to live a life that is mediocre at best
You gave Your most, let me score high on Your test

I Sing A Song Of Love To You

I sing a song of Love to You
You gave me a brand new start
I sing a song of Love to You
You came into my heart

I sing a song of Love to You
You poured Your blood for me
I sing a song of Love to You
You took my sins to Calvary

Jesus, Jesus
You are my hearts desire
Jesus, Jesus, Jesus
I want to go much higher

I sing a song of Love to You
Your Spirit true in my life
I sing a song of Love to You
You take away my strife

I sing a song of Love to You
Your forgiveness so precious to me
For You went for me to Calvary
You went for me to Calvary

Jesus, Jesus
You are my hearts desire
Jesus, Jesus, Jesus
I want to go much higher

Jesus My Friend

Do we all realize what a friend we have in Jesus
He came into life to be with us and to please us
Came to Earth to destroy the works of the evil one
Remember He didn't have to He was Gods own Son

To pray continually, to pray without ceasing
To talk with God in prayer we are releasing
Gave us a way to have a friend all of the time
Lives in us His glory like a beautiful rhyme

When we do sin He is still with us then
Waiting for us to repent turn from the sin
When life is hard and we can hardly bare it
The One inside us suffered more than a bit

So I thank Him for staying with me all the while
Being so generous and kind with love is His style
To think He took my sin into deaths grip
I feel so ashamed when in life I do slip

Then when I'm weak He carries me along
This man wants to change when doing wrong
To turn around and walk by His side
Not that I didn't enjoy the nice ride

So if you may be looking for a friend for life
Jesus is looking for a body to call His wife
For the church is His body, this is you and me
And this friendship and more is for eternity

Joy In Jesus Saving Grace

Having joy down deep in my heart
Comes along when the day does start
Joy all through the day's events
In every flower and in every scent

Beauty of the earth His glory shows
Every man that's accepted Him, knows
Jesus my lord, You gave so much to me
Not just for today but eternally

Every breath that I take, each day I do live
Your joy increases as I sing, or to another I give
Want Your touch all the days of my life through
Thank You dear Jesus at Calvary You for-knew

All the things that would happen, hardships too
When they do occur I look for the joy in You
For You are my joy, my life, and my love
Came from the Father, His Son from above

Now I pray for the others I know, they need You
For You my Savior to come through for them too
You have the control; You can hook them real good
Was when You came to me that I truly understood

So go to my loved ones the joy of my time
Asking You so simple in simple rhyme
Come to my assistance and save them as well
Your Spirit, Your Love, Your story we will tell

Just Happiness

Just happiness is all I want
Just happiness is all I need
Devil, he scares and taunts
I am a co-heir, I am Gods seed

I am seated in high places
With Christ Jesus I do sit
Seeing Him I will be like Him
Not noticing the difference a bit

He will give all the direction
By His power we will win
For sure is our election
He died for all our sin

Now I'll fight the battles on high
Fighting is in His Spirit you see
Spiritual warfare in all His might
I'll be doing, but it will not be me

Living in peace in all that I do
Fighting the battle in faith and trust
My happiness each day is anew
Cannot be bothered by moth or rust

Kisses

There are many kisses here on earth
They come in all forms even from birth
Hugs too with love being all around us
Smiles on the faces of those that we trust

As our years grow, kisses still happen in love
Mom and dad too all coming from above
Relatives as well kisses and hugs all around
Love comes to us in a sweet smelling sound

God is the giver of love in all things
Learn of His glory, the life that He brings
It is He that causes, creates all that we see
Only He can help us become all we can be

But our losses are great, pain and sorrow the more
Illness strikes in suffering and pain, at our very door
We call on God for an answer to continue our flight
Sometimes we are up and praying all night

He fills us with His Spirit, and teaches as well
The kisses you now get will cause you to tell
Whoever receives them will be the better for sure
As Jesus is always the answer and the cure

Let Our Light Be Bright

Sun rising in the morn
Beauty of creation to be seen
Light touching land, darkness torn
Life to the ocean and glistening sea

Who would know the day and night
But to watch sun rising and to set
Out to work with the coming light
Sharing the day with all those we met

Bringing home sustenance to our family life
Gathering what we will, what we can
To feed and clothe our children and wife
But its all from the Creators plan

Do we see the meaning of daylight
Do we know our true flight
Do we work with all our might
Do we have the Creator in our sight

For without our God fading light surrounds
Darkness grows throughout our days
For in the truth there are no bounds
If we will just kneel and pray

Never Say Never

We are to believe so we must believe all
The Bible is true from the first page to last
The devil will try to cause us to fall
Will bring up every negative from the past

But we believe God and in His true Word
We will never say never and trust Him true
Losers give up all walks of life, you've heard
Positive thinking brings a new day, skies blue

Believe it to be done, doubt not in your heart
Mountains will be moved, have any in your life
Then trust Jesus in what He said, begin and start
To submit to God, trust in Him and sheath your knife

The battle is His He won't let you down
Pray on your knees, pray on your face too
Then let it go from your grasp, hear the sound
Of His Spirit moving the mountain just for you

Never say never, say thank you my Lord
At peace in His rest, sing songs to His praise
While you are resting He will pull out His sword
Now see what He has done His banner you will raise

Thanking God in all He has done in your place
Living in His peace, His Spiritual blessing as well
Knowing Gods order now in each and every case
Soon you will have many testimonies to tell

Not I That Live

It is not I that live, but Christ that lives in me
These words of Paul state simply the way to be
This life I live, I live by faith in the Son of God
God created all man from the same sod

Made in His image our very breath is His
Some thinking everlasting life, chances are slim
Some think they are important, so high tech
To a believer it looks that their life is a wreck

So glad it is You that loves and controls me
I never want to be part of the walking dead
That I believe in a Savior and a higher calling
Thought of actually going to hell is appalling

Lord help me to live in Your Spirit, Your light
Sometimes it feels Your holding me tight
Show me; teach me the way of Your Love
Come Holy Spirit gentle as the dove

I pick up Your Cross my belief in Your way
You Lord I can trust each and every day
Bumpy road at times, knowing You did pave
Remember the pain and the sacrifice You gave

Sing Praise To Jesus

Songs come to me in my spirit sometimes
Poems come as well in very simple rhyme
Reading the Word will bring out my best
Hoping always that I pass the Lords test

Living life each day by believing in God
Seeing Him simply, looking for His nod
To know that He speaks to me is everything
Worship and praise to Him I do bring

Going to church, the assembling of the saints
Beauty all around and the skies that He paints
Look for yourself He is everywhere you see
Every breath that you breathe, all you can be

Choice is free now, won't always be that way
Time will come when on knees all men will pray
Listen now carefully I just want to share
I'm not pushing it on you, yet I really do care

It comes from His Spirit in me that I want you to know
If you will receive Him now a good life you will sow
More than that too, you'll have His Spirit as well
And you will be in the One, and another you will tell

That we are born to know Him; He gave us our being
Eternity and forever, this you'll be seeing
Part of the whole, finally where you belong
You too will worship and praise Him in song

Spirit From Above

All that I am and all I'll ever be
For I am nothing without Him you see
But through His grace, He'll send His dove
Will be from heaven above

It's all that I seem to want these days
This is my dream and for it I pray
Landing on me Holy Spirit in Love
That in me they'll see Jesus from above

For the needs are great in the multitude
That from His Love I'll be cued
To give to another a more important prayer
And in this I truly do care

We want you more and more dear Jesus
For you are what we need Lord Jesus
I love you Lord is all I can say
Without you I can't work, sing or pray

I love you Jesus, increasing every minute
You are the Holy Spirit I want to live in
Jesus You are my hearts desire
You are Lord God, Holy Father, and Sire

You are the King my Savior, my love
It is You from within and from above
All that I am or ever will be
You are my all and all You see

You are everything to me

To Live In You

Jesus my friend, everything to me
In living my life and all I can be
In the mountains and sky and all I can see
Hard to know they hung You on a tree

Even the ones that You loved so dear
The ones You sought and brought so near
You spoke to them without any fear
From the Word, from the past it was so clear

Yet You suffered and died for all of man
You took all the sin, it was Your plan
You opened a door as only You can
So now in You, my life will stand

By Your Spirit that You sent
I now live not swayed or bent
For You in me is what You meant
Your life being Spirit, You sent

For all of man, sometimes me too
We do not know that You are so true
For the world hasn't a clue
What it's like to live in You
We do so need more of You

Unity In Jesus In Worship

When we worship in unity His presence does fall
All in one accord, His Spirit fills the hall
Fathers Spirit is in us when we believe in His Son
We are not under the Law its ok to have some fun

We can raise our hands, for they are holy to Him
Can soak in His Spirit not going out on a limb
There is no special way if our worship is real
Keeping order in respect not making a big deal

If His Spirit is moving we might jump around
Some believe its ok to jump up and down
Just know to respect the ways where you are
When in Rome do as they do, its not that hard

But be real in your worship for God is so real
Anything at home I would say is no big deal
For Jesus said to love one another this is why
We treat each with respect in unity we will try

God is always happy when we mean what we say
He is very happy when in one accord we do pray
When we accept His Sons gift of eternal life too
He is pleased knowing He'll be forever with you

Waking With You Lord

When I wake in the morning, I think of You Lord
Getting up to go I need my armor and my sword
How could anything else be in my thoughts but You
For You come to me each morning, Your presence so true

Come be with me Holy Spirit as I start each day
Talking with You Lord, we talk and I pray
For the evil on this earth is nothing new
The devil like a roaring lion, He's in the mix too

Jesus when You died You defeated him well
The gospel going forth into the world to tell
You tricked the evil one, opening the door
Holy of Holies draperies, from top to bottom tore

A new covenant between God and man, good news
To become believers, all of creation, no cost, no dues
Free offering of salvation to all mankind on earth
Into the body of God, all of man offered a new birth

Leaving behind sin and the ways of evil a must
Over time, we learn that truly in God we can trust
When we fail, we are quick to seek God and repent
Door now open to the Father is why He was sent

Receive now my friends and all that might read this
Like going to bed, and mom and dads good night kiss
Relationship with God, better than any preacher says
Like breakfast on the table and Gods beautiful days

Many days gone by knowing You so well
Still not knowing all that You are to tell
Yet, I live each day now trusting in Your Word
I'm so glad You sent it and grateful that I heard

We Worship You Lord Jesus

We worship You Jesus with all our heart
With our mind and strength we worship You
We sing songs to You Jesus from the days start
You sacrificed for us and we know it's true

You're worthy of worship and songs galore
You have made a way for us to have fullness of joy
You're worthy of praise when we walk out the door
You opened the way for every girl and boy

We have a life with You as Your friends
We live in Your Spirit, in our soul, in our heart
We leave behind, traditions and trends
No matter our condition we have a new start

Give our teachers Your wisdom to teach
Give our workers Your strength to bear it
Give our preachers Your Spirit to preach
Give into our life the desire share it

Now let us be the body of Christ
Use us as Your own to show Your way
Double anointing, anoint us twice
We'll show in our life, You're here to stay

Holy Spirit come upon us as we worship in truth
Use us as Your own to show Your true way
Let us praise You Jesus in all that we do
And in Your Holy Sprit is where we will stay

We worship You Jesus, we worship You

Your Presence

Father we come to Your throne room
We call on Your name above all names
From death into life from the tomb
All other ways are just like games

We know Your presence will come near
Come Holy Spirit fall upon us now
We turn away from evil and fear
We will connect to You somehow

Saturate Your people with Your love
Speak to our hearts in our need today
Living Spirit descend from above
Come into our hearts and stay

Father we stand in joy before You
To give praise to only You alone
Your presence our reward in all we do
We build up in You our cornerstone

Fall upon us Your people in Your Spirit
We stand in awe, Your glory and fame
Still small voice, let us hear it
Oh God set us on fire by Your flame

ABOUT GOD, JESUS, HIS SPIRIT AND SALVATION

Beginning And End

I am the Alpha and Omega, beginning and the End
I am Father God, Jesus all of mans best friend
I am the Groom to return to receive my beautiful bride
I'm speaking of My Church all the saints by my side

When I return my heart will be full of vengeance and Love
A trumpet will ring and the sky will open from above
Be ye ready for I will come like a thief in the night
To those who believe what a beautiful sight

There is usually another chance but I say the time is near
I don't want you to fret My perfect Love will drive out fear
Just know that I Love you and for you gave My own life
It's the greatest thing I Myself could do for My wife

So clean yourself up put on your robe of true joy
For your God, I Jesus am coming for just you solely
I am your all in all and I Love all mankind
My justice will be fair to all true in their time

Now speak to yourself do you want to come with Me
I offered the free gift, laid My life down, hung on a tree
The time is so near I now reach My heart just to you
Please accept My life as a reason to believe true

I'm coming for You

Believe In God And Me

Morning comes, thoughts stumbling in my mind
Lost arrangements and where is the time
From the outer edge coming to the core
It seems there should be so much more

Ah yes, appointments now I must arise
For the day awaits for those that are wise
Accomplishments yes today I will pursue
For society wants surely its dues

Now I am moving coffee within me
Opportunity is knocking and there I'll be
For time wasted is behind me now
Now the future ahead and I know how

Tomorrow I will awake thoughts on the move
When the sun arises this I will prove
For within me I believe in me
I believe in God, I believe in me

Breezes

The soft smell within the breeze whisking by
Tickles my nose with the fresh morning dew
Taking a deep breath the clean air is why
I see Him in the morning and the evening too

As the day goes on I think of the thickness of air
As I breathe the life giving air so alive as it seems
Going home after the day to my family, I so care
All ready to meet me, couldn't be better in a dream

Sitting on the porch swing the sun is moving to set
Colors are beginning to appear like a painting of God
It was a day like this very one, the day that we met
I asked Him to look down to me and His head did nod

The sky still changing swirling strokes, beauty reaching
Changing of color is like seeing a miracle beginning to
glow
Then deepening into darkness like a lesson He's teaching
As I noticed the light was still bright down in my soul

And so each day brings the glory of God to me
From morning to darkness He's all around to see
Then the breezes are gently moving the leaves in trees
I know God is showing Himself, I feel Him in the breeze

Come Lord, live with us

Life longing for God to assist
The more I learn the more to resist
More accountable to all I do
In His love I can pursue
I can do nothing without You
Jesus please, I've been through so much
When I move and just be I need Your touch
For the devil is trying to destroy
In pain and sickness so little to enjoy
I can do nothing without You
God, Father I ask in Jesus name
All sin at Calvary I should have no shame
I feel without You I can't go on
In Your Spirit, with grace, a little fun?
I can't make it without You
Resisting the devil and he should flee
Only in submission to You, all Holy
Gods building this body, Jesus the Head
Resurrected is He, no longer dead
I can do nothing without Him

Country Drive

Took a ride out of the city vibes
Stress level high on every side
Leaving town traffic was slowing
My peace in God ever growing

Pecan trees for miles on end
Straight always and a few bends
Sunlight shining through the trees
Like a strobe effect is what I see

Slowing a bit, relaxing the more
Good thoughts down to my core
Still small voice I begin to hear
Into His Spirit becoming clear

City forgotten seems long ago
Singing to God feeling aglow
His presence now filling the car
He is now with me not so far

I love You Lord, thank you Jesus
You always just want to ease us
I should travel to country more
Always open is Gods front door

Do You Believe

Do you believe in God
That He created all of all
Do you pray at your meal
Is He Supreme being for real

Is Jesus His only Son
Are we all Sons of God
Did He send Him here
Is His Spirit very near

Do you see the world so sad
Do you believe that Jesus is God
Is your heart happy this day
Are you willing to knell and pray

Do you want some more evidence
Have you asked Him to show you
What would it take for you to believe
If He's real will you be relieved

If your relieved and His gift is free
If Jesus took the sins of the world to death
If Jesus is the Son of God
Opened heavens door and said come in

Just take His gift, if you notice no change
Then you may have a reason to say no
Yet if His offer is true and you say yes
Be happy, in Spirit you shall grow

Faces

Standing in the crowd faces about me
Music is fine everyone seems happy
Anointed singing such a joy to hear
Some of the songs are even snappy

Pastor prays and enjoys his work
Gives a message, the point is clear
Some are stirred, in emotions and mind
Peoples faces showing a little fear

Conclusion of message heard by all
Some are squirming, not moving a bit
Spirit of God now takes His place
Faces with sin just wanting to split

Question comes now loud and clear
Knowing in self if He is speaking to you
To make the decision, to repent or defer
Wondering if anyone even has a clue

Some faces bow some look ahead
Will it change anyone in the Makers plan
Speaking to God for now is the time
Or some to stay so proud and just stand

Face up or face down, to rationalize or be true
For leaving this place now, One will know
To live in denial or to face up to your God
Spirit in your heart does now show

Feelings

When you think the creator of earth and man
Is He spirit or physical that you see in your eye
Did you know Him before; are you part of His plan
When you think of His Love, do you begin to cry

Do you see Him from mind or see Him from heart
Has He become your friend in this life that you live
Did you hear of Him from bible, how did it start
When He gave up His life, just what did He give

If the Creator is His Father and Spirit is He
And His mother is of flesh, conceived by Him
Jesus, Son of man, Spirit and flesh He will be
He showed us true life, filled our cup to the brim

To take all the sin from past, present, and future
This received to Jesus, then to take them to death
A final sacrifice He made, for mankind to be nurtured
Beaten, whipped, put on a cross, He took His last breath

Many feelings about this man; and who was He
From Loved to hated, yet He offered for free
If He is the Son of God, could we all try to see
To receive His gift, gives us life eternally

Back to our Creator, in His image we are made
Back home as it were, He has shown us the way
To receive Your gift Lord, on this day we pray
That we may return to You and there we will stay

Forever Building

We evaluate our life by the things we acquire
Our home, our land, our hands create and inspire
Do we have more than the man down the street
Gathering our money, oh the smell is so sweet

Building our bodies, minds filled with knowledge
Graduation at last, we are finished with college
We marry and we mate, our children, the best
Oh our ancestors before, our own families crest

Secure in our pride, we can care for our own
Filling our cupboards, our dog has a bone
Our life now complete, feels it will never end
Thinking of death now, away thought! I send

Middle age now here, was that a pain in my neck
Pains in the back, tired at night, oh what the heck
Doctor my friend, did I hear right, what did you say
No hope my dear wife, do you think we should pray

Fifties, I made it and my finances are secure
Spiritual life, knowing not how, not being sure
What I need now I can't build nor can I buy
Needing Gods mercy and touch I begin to cry

Hard heart I have, can't really feel His love
Still seeming to know He's caring from above
Wishing I would have taken the time to inquire
Spent more time, letting His Spirit inspire

Have read His words and believe them to be true
Believing in resurrection, morning sun on the dew
Spirit strengthens as wisdom comes along with age
Everlasting life, only Jesus, only one, set the stage

Forgiveness

Our words need much more attention
Some of them hurt, don't speak them or mention
For pain deep in the heart can cut like a knife
Lets watch our words, each husband and wife

A good saying to be true, if you forgive,
God will forgive you
He will forgive you in the same measure
that you forgive too
Truthfully, judging comes close when we do not forgive
Judge not, you shall be judged in the same manner
as you live

Look at the sin not at the person; maybe they
will do the same
Then maybe we can all live in peace and no one will blame
We were not even among the saved till Christ gave His life
Grafted into the vine, being one of His own, a real life

The Lord judges all; it is His and His decision alone
Our understanding is the measuring tape for Him to atone
Not by keeping the standard of another,
will you reach your goal
If this is your way, you might end up paying a toll,
possibly your soul

Let us lift another higher than ourselves,
esteem him higher too
Let us help the widows and children that are alone,
yes you!
Church on Sunday will help you make your way,
in your praise
The Word of God will settle in too, all of man it can save

Overall, it's living a life with a relationship with the Lord
It's fighting your fights with softness and
a two edged sword
It's knowing Him so well, deciding on His direction
He gives to you freely, praise Him, Love His mention

Let us decide to follow His ways
Let us do it for the rest of our days
Let us continually, constantly pray
Give Him our life to make His own today

Forgive Them Lord They Know Not What They Do

We are all sinners don't be so blind
We are all the same, it shines like a sign
Some think they're better some realize not
We all must see for a price we were bought

So, don't judge another when sin resides in you
This is true of a Christian or a Jew
In all other religions, the result is the same
But don't feel so bad for you are not to blame

If you're judging, another by mans own thoughts
You'll end up in sin when you really should not
We are all created in the very image of God
He made all individuals from the same sod

It's a choice we have to make simple and true
Do we want to please God in all that we do
If this is so receive peace from Gods Son
He did everything that could possible be done

He took all the sin to the cross in His death
He was faithful and true till His very last breath
He loves you so much, He did this for you
Something you couldn't possibly do

Just accept this gift from the Creator of man
Think all this thru, if its possible you can
For heaven or hell awaits us all just the same
Forgive them oh Lord, in Jesus Your name

HIS SPIRIT WILL HELP ME

Hope Of Our Calling

Without hope the world looks so dim
Seems our success in the world is slim
We hear of a hope that is greater for sure
Everlasting life would help in our cure

Positive thinking is proven to work well
Where does it come from, should I tell
All things come from God, did you know
For when we accept Him hope does grow

Find salvation in Christ the hope of glory
For friends around you testify of your story
To walk and talk with your Creator each day
Relationship will grow with Him you shall stay

He's calling your name to put in the book of life
Heed to His call bring your family and wife
For God knew you from the day of your birth
There is no better call you may receive on earth

Share these words with all that you know
Open the Book and with the words do show
That Jesus Christ is the Son of God true
I hear the call now; here it's for you

Holy Spirit Please Lead

Why do we worry about letting Gods Spirit lead
Are we afraid we won't be able to meet His need
Do we think we will bring confusion to our midst
When in reality His Spirit only brings in bliss

We think I say that it will get out of our hand
We are afraid that our emotions will take a stand
Are we really afraid that we are not able to deliver
Do we think His Spirit will only make us quiver

That goose bumps will make us feel that He is here
We want the service to be in order as we really do care
That, what is seen in our gatherings is only from Him
The Word is safe, it is truth, we shall study and trim

But what if we really let Holy Spirit take His lead
Is it possible that we would fulfill more of our need
Holy Spirit was given to help us guide into praise
He will join with us, a Spiritual standard He will raise

Let us not worry about church being out of control
For if we do, it shall bring forth a large and dead toll
Open your mind; surely you can move out of His way
Not by might nor by power but by His Spirit He will stay

God wants to pour His Spirit upon man
We must be open and know that He truly can
Get out of the way and let Him now lead
He will surprise you and fill all of your need

I Can Do Nothing Without You

Life longing for God to assist
The more I learn the more to resist
More accountable to all I do
In Your Love I can pursue
I can do nothing without You

Jesus please, I've been through so much
When I move and just be I need Your touch
For the devil is trying to destroy
In pain and sickness so little to enjoy
I can do nothing without You

God, Father, I ask in Jesus name
All sin at Calvary I should have no shame
I feel without You I can't go on
In Your Spirit with grace, a little fun
I can't make it without You

Resisting the devil and he should flee
Only in submission to You all Holy
Gods building this body, Jesus the head
Resurrected was He, no longer dead
I can do nothing without You

Jesus Said

I am the way the truth and the life
Come to Me and give Me your strife
Submit and believe and you'll be saved
You don't even have to be brave

Reach by faith and receive Me now
My Spirit will live in you; I'll show you how
Read My word and day by day
I'll show you how to live My way

Come to Me each day and pray
And in your heart I'll promise to stay
Listen to Me, I'll speak in your ear
In My perfect love you have nothing to fear

Talk to Me for I am your friend
Worry not of what you did or where you've been
For I gave my life to wash you clean
For all sin done and all sin seen

One more thing to you I'll say
Trust in Me when you work or play
When all you've done is all you can do
I'll be the one who carries you through

I Love You

Jesus Is The Way

Hard to understand why Jesus is the way
Which church is right where should I stay
Many religions on earth all around to see
Then some take and change Christianity

Trying to find the answers by study and plan
Without the Lord there is no where to stand
Science is beating down Gods own earth
Ignoring all together the virgin birth

If all religions sound near the same
It makes it mostly, mans own game
If they all came around long long ago
To give us all a reason to live and know

It's hard to believe that Jesus is the only way
So we must with intellect explain and pray
When so many other religions say, they are right
Than our answer will come only by His might

And leaving it there only He can please us
And who's to say God didn't do it by Jesus
Not hard to understand when you see it by faith
Nothing to achieve just receive Him this day

Living In Jesus

Like a little child at any age
Once you're saved your life begins
You read the book page by page
For Jesus died to cover your sins

A babe, a child, a teen, a man
Growing a bit day by day
I'll get to heaven I know I can
For my Jesus has the last say

Now that I've grown, so far yet to go
I know of the stages of life's pain
And Jesus I'll follow this I know
And with Him forever I'll reign

This poem was written about 25 years ago at
The time when I received Christ. It was short
Yet to the point. I actually grew up in a religious
Family but truly started my relationship with the
Lord at about this time. I was ready.

Love Of God

Believe the Bible, states that God is love
And His Spirit resides within our heart
We begin to notice His Spirit from above
No longer the same from the morning start

With all mankind we see love all around
Mother holding her baby can feel the joy
Brilliant blue sky, to earths' good ground
Loving all Gods creation, much to enjoy

Praying for our enemies, loving one another
Loving Jesus His Son, Father loving us as well
Without love there is no church, sister or brother
Nothing is profit without love the Bible does tell

Love does not envy, suffers long and is kind
Not provoked, puffed up, no parade, no envy tale
Bears, believes, endures, hopes all things, why
Rejoices in truth not sin, thinks no evil, never fails

Of faith hope and love, love being God, the best
Walking in the Light, Spirit, Love, in His Truth
Book of Life to be opened, did we pass His test
Name written down, Lord Jesus, joy in the proof

Married And Living Married

Smile at each other when you wake
Do you do it for the other ones sake
Are you doing it to have a better day
Or doing it so you may be able to play

Do you love your mate or self the more
Do you want to make him or her to soar
Will you try and hear the other this time
To sit on the bed is not much of a climb

Breakfast maybe they would like it in bed
Make your move now enough has been said
Do it today take some time to show your love
For love is from God and it comes from above

Taking an extra moment, worthwhile time spent
For to the other half it might be a big time event
Go on a holiday, go to lunch, if only a long drive
Pack a sandwich or stop, will make both feel alive

One more thing if you really want a super day
Pray together to God that He will direct your way
His Spirit will guide, be with you and in you as well
When you get back you will have a great story to tell

Missing You Jesus

Lord Jesus I've read from Your book of Love
I believe that You Lord did come from above
I believe that Father God was pleased with your life
I believe You were sinless and took no wife

I've prayed on my knees, and prayed on my face
I've done my best to repent and run a good race
I accepted You as my savior and believe You are God
I know You brought grace instead of the rod

I've wanted to know You much closer each day
I talk to You while I work, and while I play
I thank You when I am happy and when I am down
I know my physical comes from the ground

I know that I walk with Your Spirit within me
I know that in heaven is where I will be
Yet I have never been able to hold Your hand
To look into Your eyes while we make our plan

To know the sound of Your talk and Your walk
To hear your laughter and to see Your smile
To watch You work with Your power from above
To give You a hug and physically feel Your Love

Yet I talk to You from morning till night
I know You are true and give us true light
Will You let me know You as much as I can
In this day, on this earth Your face to this man

I miss You without touching You except in my heart
I miss You like when a love one must part
Oh Jesus I miss You come close to me now
Share Your gifts and show me Your smile
I miss You Lord

Outside the Boundaries

There is a place outside the boundaries of mind
There it seems people seek spirit of some kind
Meditation in ceasing the mental activity, done
To gain a touch of another realm, to some

Prayer of all kinds to seek the same place
All of religions and self seeking in the race
To find a peace and the hope to live on
Fleeing from death seems that all men run

To take the step from mind to the spirit
All kinds of ceremonies trying to get near it
Some call it God and try to emerge with Him
Following every new thing and every whim

And many do get to the place where they feel it
Making themselves peaceful and not to fear it
Looking to Buddha and nirvana and such
Eastern religions and most others say they can touch

But the thing is as I've studied most of the ways
I tried another and another, with one I couldn't stay
I felt the spirit and peace from within me
But none did much to really change what I see

I decided to go with Jesus in a great need was I
I hoped I found something that would answer the why
I gave my life and prayed the sinners prayer too
But actually a relationship, no I had not a clue

So I studied His Word and prayed so sincere
I wanted to find Him and to see Him real clear
Again I found the place of peace within my being
So I took the Word and tried life without the seeing

But a strange thing happened, it wasn't just for me
Suddenly I noticed that others looked and did see
That something had changed; I was no longer the same
I truly did believe, it was no longer a game

And the peace that I was seeking was truly in me
Only thing was it wasn't just for me to see
It went through me and I shared it with another
And as He moved through me I gained a brother

Now Jesus lives in me, His presence is real now
He loves me I know and His Spirit is how
I love Him too and His people as well
And for the rest of my life His story I will tell

So I'll tell you now my friend who may read this
I don't need to seek and search to find that bliss
I have it inside; Jesus lives and directs me all the time
I hope as you read this He'll save you with
words that rhyme

Jesus is Lord, He is real, and He is true
He died at Calvary for me and you
So accept this from Him, it is free
And forever you'll live in eternal harmony

Perfect Love Drives Out Fear

God is Love this is a fact
His life He gave that we may act
He died to save us, took our sin
To receive His grace and become His kin

We live our life in earth's great pain
That in the end we'll have great gain
Needing to see Him again, our eyes to see
To be in attendance with Him in glee

As the wars rage and good men die
We pray and pray and then we cry
For Satan has his reign for a time, we see
He'll take away what we are meant to be

He'll try to get us by any means
Keep us involved in our minds and needs
However, in our heart this is for sure
There is a Jesus and He is the cure

For He's already calling our name
Its good to realize there is no blame
To open our hearts to His Spirit always
Living water He'll give us all of our days

We are no longer blind but now we see
That Jesus died for all, even you and me
Thank you Jesus, make us all we can be
I see, I see, I see, I see!

Prayer Is Worldwide

Most of the world will bow to their knees
To pray to a God to fill all their needs
They try to reach outside the boundaries of life
To worship their God and move away from strife

Religions are many; they all think they're right
As they pray and pray with all of their might
To ask the Creator for a better way to live
Many of them, their very life they will give

Yet all the religions say near the same thing
They pray and worship and dance and sing
Not understanding or seeing their God
Just wanting Him to give them the nod

That they may think there is more life to be
That if they pray enough some of it they may see
The presence of God here on our good earth
More to life than just death and their birth

That their family will not end with the sting of death
That it isn't over when we breathe our last breath
That God will save us from the death that we see
That after our death our existence will still be

Most religions offer some kind of spiritual touch
But to see beyond death, we see not too much
So we must rely on mans science and knowledge
We learn in school, and then it's on to college

But all of the knowledge and things that we learn
And all the prayer and touch of God we do yearn
Will not take us to where we are filled up
We will still end up with half of the cup

But there is a way; God didn't leave us without
Through Abraham's faith, He brought Jesus about
Now by faith in our prayer to believe in Him
Will give us a life full and life that will not end

Seems too simple for most to accept as true
But in reality there has been many a clue
So read the bible and you too can see
There is an answer that lasts an eternity

So let us not worry about all those who pray
If they don't yet know Jesus He may give them a way
Now as you are praying pray for the entire world too
For salvation is for all, not just me and you

There is nothing impossible for God to do
Let us have faith and let Him be true
Share where you can and live your life for Him
And do you very best to stay away from sin

Do not judge anyone that you meet
Forgive all of man in church or on the street
Let God be God we can't outdo His plan
Just in your own life for Him make your stand

Now Jesus I pray You will make a way for all
Of the men and woman who pray and to You call
Touch our hearts and let us not think we are pure
Only You God, Lord Jesus can really give the cure

It's hard to finish for many are of the lost
And I have a hard time thinking of the cost
Of what You gave, Your life sacrificed that day
That many more than we think will make it I pray

The final decision is Yours this is sure
You are the Creator and You will endure
Help us oh God we are but just men
You created us both man and woman

Sin Cleansing

The wages of sin are death
Man would have his last breath
Many sacrifices were made to God
He ruled with a strong rod

They sinned over and over again
Through the centuries more sin
He threw His strong rod
They fell into the sod

From God the Messiah to come
Prophets spoke to some
They fell on their knees
Forgive us oh God, please

A hope was in the wind
A way to take away sin
Answer was to come
Gods only Son

Finally the savior did come
Brought with Him a New Kingdom
Loving one another
Stranger and brother

He was without sin you see
So He took our sin to the tree
In His death, He took our sin
And all sin that has been

Sin now gone, He opened the door
His name is Jesus, need you know more
If you try to do it alone chances are slim
Wisdom is to believe in HIM

The Fruits From Jesus To Me

My Love is in your power
Resurrected from Calvary
My joy is in overcoming
Jesus is my victory

My peace is in Your Spirit
You gave this gift to me
My patience is in Your sorrows
You've worked it into me

My gentleness is from Your heart
A touch from You into me
My kindness Your compassion gave me
That others may truly see

Your goodness in deeds, in truth
Conformed to Your image, I'll be
My faithfulness by no works
A measure You gave to me

Self control now in my life
In my mouth, my actions, my being
Clean me white as snow dear Lord
Pour Your precious blood on me

Work Your fruits into me Lord
That You in me they'll see
Jesus, Jesus, Jesus
You're everything to me

Three In One

There is God the Father, God the Son
God the Holy Ghost and they're all One
They planned the Creation of earth together
Jesus will be the One to come down and gather

When we receive Jesus Holy Spirit is inside
If we follow Him close we'll have a good ride
Jesus, conceived from Spirit the Fathers own seed
Half Spirit and half man is what the world did need

He was subjected to all needs the same as man
Except Jesus did not sin as all of mankind can
He was obedient to the Father to the very end
Had all of temptation yet He did not sin

He is our Savior, our brother and our friend
All of mans sin beginning to end, He did mend
He is all that I mentioned and so very much more
For He died at Calvary to open to heaven a door

Just to say yes to His call in your life
Work hard; love your children and wife
Fervently pray for all your problems and needs
Pass the good news about Jesus down to your seed

Who Is God

Is God a figment of our imagination
Is He just something we need to exist
Were we created in His very own image
Or did we come from the sea and its mist

Are we to create a God as people do each day
Yes we'll try to search all we know and think
Shall we read everything written about Him
Will we ourselves begin to write by pen and ink

Do any of us know more than we can learn
Is there anyplace we can go to find a hidden note
How can we believe in something we can't see
Will we ever be able to submit an all-knowing vote

Some pray to break through, through the day and eve
Others will believe in what they find inside their self
Somehow a connection must be made to believe
Or we will take the whole notion and place it on a shelf

Oh God who can know of Your ways and worth
So many religions on this world round and round
We fight to say we have the history and truth
Tell me which way will take me heaven bound

Now we know Jesus was on earth, lived and died
Said He was the Son of God told us of His way
To reach true standing and place with the creator
His message took Him to the grave, but He did not stay

He came back from deaths sting, said to follow Him
To believe in His resurrection forever we shall live
He rose from the dead, all the others went dim
Gave His life, seems the best one can offer or give

Why Jesus

Looking at the world and its prophets through time
We can believe in them all and not commit a crime
From Buddha, Mohammad and all other leaders as such
Each of their teachings has merit but where is the touch

Each lived here on earth and taught some good things
They each lived their life learning what life brings
But which of them said he was the Son of the Creator
Which one said he was mans friend and his Savior

Now with Jesus it is said, came through a virgin birth
Never has this happened from the beginning of earth
Old Testament was written through four thousand years
A Messiah was coming to wipe away the hurts and tears

He came to earth to free man of hopelessness and sin
The present, the future and of all sin that had been
Was all loaded upon Him as He took His last breath
Never sinning Himself, He took it all to His death

Resurrected from the grave His death didn't last
Different from the other prophets of the past
He lived again, gifted the same for all man
Just say you believe and mean it if you can

POEMS – CHILDREN

Boy And His Sister With Stuffies

You want to play with bear and dog
Ok bear says while sitting on a log
Growl is you scared my little friend
Bark Bark I'll chase you around the bend

Lets just walk and be friends ok
Ok then lets just go and play
Look some honey said the bear
A bee bit me one time I'm scared

Don't be scared dog God will protect us
Listen bear in God you have to trust
I'm a boy and I'm the bear so there
Well I'm the girl bark bark I don't care

I can pray just as hard as you bear boy
You know that dog is really just a toy
Growl grrrrrrr so do I scare you now
Oh I'm so scared oh my, wow

Hi mister dog I really don't want to fight
Ok you big bear lets try to make it right
Sis I love you and God does too
Brother you're the best, God and me love you

Childs Faith

A Childs faith is as simple as can be
When you tell them of God they see
When you tuck them in they see love
They believe it is in you and from above

They don't question if He lives or not
Feeling our love, all they ever sought
So when the world tells them wrong
They still hear a beautiful song

Jesus loves me yes I know this is true
I hope that you know Him more too
He is everywhere can't you see
Oh my gosh look at that tree

He made that tree and that flower too
He made everything and he made you
Have Jesus in your heart you'll be ok
You will be happy all of the day

My little darling its time for bed
Come hug me mom, kiss my head
Come on now dad I need a hug too
Mom and dad and Jesus I love you.

Childs Simple Prayer To God

I love You so much, because you made me
Thank you for creating the world I see
Help make me good for mom and dad
Help me to never be real bad

Father You are the reason I live
I get lots of things and You help me to give
If it wasn't for You the world wouldn't be good
Kids are mean, I wish they understood

Big people are mean too and war is killing
I don't think they know You or get the right feeling
I wish they would talk to You like I do Jesus
Cause I know You really just want to just please us

I think we do what You want us to do
Why can't we all play, and be happy too
Why don't you just tell us now all that You can
Cause big people don't want to just play in the sand

So I ask You Jesus to bring back the good here
Cause then in all of us You will be so near
Everyone will know how nice that You are
They will come to You from near and far

Then we can play with You all of the day
The world will be better, this I pray
The wars and crying will stop right then
Cause when You come there will be no more sin

Everybody Up Its Time For Breakfast

Come and eat every one of you now
Your Daddy's going to have a cow
What's for breakfast can I have pancakes
Its eggs and bacon make no mistake

Oh gee Mom can I have some cereal
It's really, like Mom its no big deal
Everyone is eating the same
I cooked it all this is no game

Hurry now Daddy's ready to drive away
He won't leave us Mom I'm ready anyway
Come on kids get in the car
If you don't hurry up the walk will be far

Your Mom will pick you up today
Don't think that it's ok to play
She'll be on time has some places to go
And you know she drives real slow

By now Dad I love you to the mountain
Love you too, no lips on the drinking fountain
Thanks Dad for the ride
Got to go now go inside

Love you Dad; love you too
See you later after school
Remember kids its ok to pray
Just do it to yourself though the day

Happy Birthday Jesus

This is the time of year we all enjoy
The bright lights are all around us to see
Much Joy for every little girl and boy
Near time to go find a lovely tree

Loving one another with our thoughts and gifts
Spending much more than we ever should
Hoping some of us will even mend the rifts
Showing our children it is good to be good

Then Santa is at the department store and malls
People bustling all around, checkbook in hand
Decorating the house, our tree and the walls
Such a good job we did, it's so very grand

Coming closer to the day of Christmas
Driving the streets to see the lights
Loving smiles, in the air, all around us
We seem to be at our best, so bright

Early that morning, did Santa arrive, yes great
Did we get all we wanted, that we did ask
Mommy the cookies and milk, Santa ate
So very happy, in love we do bask

Children, remember why we have Christmas
Jesus born on earth, that is why we celebrate
We're happy it's Jesus birthday for he lives in us
And that is for sure why Christmas is so great

I Love Mom and Teddy

I love my Mom and I love my teddy
When we go somewhere we are all ready
Put clothes on teddy, he's coming along
Him and I are going to sing a song

Mom can we go get breakfast now
I want to be big like you somehow
No darling you must go to school
You will learn a lot it will be so cool

Did you bring my lunch is it with you
Yes I have it right here it's ready too
You do everything right you are so smart
Oh darling I have God with me in my heart

Is Jesus really in me in my heart Mommy dear
Yes He is my honey when you laugh or shed a tear
Do you ever cry cause He is living in you too
Many times my sweetie when I'm happy to have you

Here we are, guess I better get out and run
Be a good student at recess have some fun
Will Jesus protect me when I'm playing ball
If you get hurt go to the nurse give me a call

See you after school I love sooo much
I love you the same, bunches and bunches
Hi honey I'm here did you have a good day
Jesus was with me I didn't get hurt as we played

Love You To Gods Moon

Morning mom, we having pancakes for breakfast today
Can we after we eat go outside, you swing me and we play
Sure honey here's some orange juice to make you strong
Ok mom while we eat can we sing a good song

Jesus loves me yes I know, mommy the Bible tells me so
That was fun and I'm all done, I want to play can we go
Its so fun for you to swing me, I love you mommy dear
You're the best that's happened to me said mom,
that's clear

Mommy I love you to the mountains and back
I love you to the mountains and around the world in fact
Well I love you too you make my heart swell
You are the best story that I'll ever hear or tell

Do you love me to the mountains and back like me
I love you to the mountains and all the way to the sea
Lets go sit down dear I'm going to tell you a story
It's about your grandpa and I, before he went to glory

I said to him one day I love you to the mountains
He said I love you too lets go to the soda fountain
We sat there drinking our soda and he sang me a tune
I love you so much my child, I love you to Gods moon

Nite Nite One More Hug

Come on sweetie its time to go to bed
Can I have some ice cream instead
No honey sandman's waiting on you
Is he going to visit you and mom too

Are you comfy is your pillow-fluffed just right
Give me a hug dad come and hold me tight
One more hug dad I love you so much, I do
After our prayers another hug for you

Lord we come to You in Jesus name tonight
Thank You for our life You help us live it right
Thank You for our life and the beautiful world we see
Thank You Jesus You are good as can be

Please help dad and mom in every single day
Help me too cause I love You, and I pray
You are in my heart all the day through
Be with me Jesus in every thing I do

Please help me to have good dreams
How about cookies and ice cream
I always brush my teeth so I think its ok
Jesus please stay with me all night and all day
Hug, Hug, one more Hug

Walking My Dog

I was walking my dog one day, he stopped
He saw a cat the bone in his mouth, he dropped
He growled and crouched real low serious as can be
The cat just looked at him like he couldn't hear or see

I pulled my dog; he picked up his bone time for us to go
Walking alone oh my, he wants to stop by a pole
Did his business oh what a day were back on our way
Oh God let us have a good walk for this I hope and pray

Doggy barked again, this time he saw another dog
The other barked just as fierce, he was chained to a log
I pulled him tight, he pulled on me a bit of tug of war
I snagged my pant leg on a bush, a little bit it tore

So I decided to jog awhile my dog loved it true
So we jogged around the block, his name was Blue
I said come on blue we're going home, hope you had fun
Felt good to me as well got myself a little sun

Oh my gosh he's running now, around the block again
I am stuck so I jogged with him same place we had been
Wasn't so bad got some good exercise but Blue looked sad
We were in the house and he remembered the fun we had

He was real happy though cause I sat him down at my feet
I reached into my happy bag and brought out a doggy treat
He enjoyed it so lying on the floor below me
I smiled at him for I was also happy as can be

GRACE AND FAITH

Cross-Grace-Faith

My faith is alive by His Grace
He died on that hilltop place
His death a sacrifice for all man
His eye was on us in His plan

I wish I could convey to you
He also died for you too
Let His death not go in vain
The sin of the world, His pain

He was sinless in nature to the end
Obedient was He for all of His kin
Created all man and woman you see
Took our place, sacrificed on that tree

It's by Grace we can all be saved
Not a thing we can add to that day
A free gift, our Creator gave, His Son
Opened a door to heaven for everyone

Open your eyes and see the way
Choose Gods Son this very day
Through that door you will go
Time will come to open and show

Your name in the book of life
In the presence of God, no strife
Forever to live in all of His Glory
Created to share it, this is our story

Faith

We must have faith to walk in Christ
We must have faith to even have hope
We want more of it asking God quite often
For if we have it, our stress will soften

Even when we think we are in His all
Somehow doubt drifts in, it will call
Where is He we say, oh where is He today
For our life's song, seems to stop its play

So once again, we are on our knees
Seeking His face, trying to please
Everything seems hard, seems so wrong
We go to Him, sing Him another song

We listen so quietly for that still small voice
We don't want another way; He's our only choice
Silence surrounds us, not even a peep
Just one word, oh we could reap

Did I hear You just now, was that You Lord
Help me dear Jesus, in you, in one accord
Without You I'm nothing, nothing at all
Oh Father in Heaven do You hear my call

Please help me now; I can't go on this way
In Your presence, I want to stay
Trusting You in the stillness of night
Giving You Lord my strength, my might

Strengthen my way show me the path
Set my feet firmly, no more wrath
Hold me now in Your Loving arms
Touch my heart allow no more harm

Faith Alive

Faith without works is dead
Works alone are dead too
Faith can move mountains
When a man is steadfast and true

Relationship with God comes by faith
To believe in One who can't be seen
Creation of earth and of man is near perfect
By some kind of force or some kind of being

Most think there must be a higher power
It couldn't all have occurred by chance
Maybe a big boom scattering matter is it
And the stars are now in some kind of dance

But I say and believe that God is the creator
Placed each star in place and then He did name
Threw them out like one spreading a blanket
They spread and expanded both violent and tame

Now man is made in His image, Jesus too
Son of God came to complete the creation
Took the sin from the world from every man
Gave faith to receive Him, to become His relation

Faith is alive if you choose to believe
A new life will come upon you this day
In the midst of the pain, suffering and such
You can receive the Joy of the Lord, OK?

Make Him your savior today

Find Jesus

Just to think that we all must die
Makes us want to know why
Just to know there is no way out
We really don't want to pout

But everyone we know leaves us someday
And after they're gone not a word to say
No one comes back to tell us a thing
Yet they tell us we should rejoice and sing

We search our minds and thoughts a lot
Its hard to think we will just lay and rot
We try to get to a spiritual place
And life continues its fast paced race

Our youth feels like it could never end
As years go we look at what we've been
Midlife seems to continue the same
Looking at everything it seems a game

The question is did we find a reason
Did we find Jesus in our life season
Is there a God who caused all this
Or are we to go into deaths dark kiss

Hold On To Your Faith

Hold on to your faith, he's coming back
It seems to be very close prophesy tells
Earthquakes and wars and rumors of more
Like sky showing rain we see what's in store

Love of many is growing cold this is for sure
Many leaving the faith, think science is the cure
Disasters all over the earth, on news everyday
Let the ones in God get on their knees and pray

For evil is rising and people turn their head
Don't look to the flesh, look to spirit instead
Eyes are getting blinded truth is now rare
Money and flesh Lord God help them care

Let it rain on man and clean up the soul
For the way of man now taking its toil
Come Lord fill the Church with Your Spirit
Give Your gift to man all Holy, let us hear it

Jesus Is Real

Jesus is real this is for sure
Question, is He all of mans cure
Everyone knows He lived indeed
But is it true, His words His creed

He offers everything He has for free
Opened a door to Heaven for you and me
As with everything there was a cost
He paid it Himself hanging on the cross

Look around you for earth is unkind
Everything we gain is only for a time
We think we have come to some great place
But in our life there's still no grace

Each of us has our own way to believe
From all we're taught looking back to retrieve
We form our thoughts, believe as we will
Most think its better to love than to kill

Seek Him and you shall find Him
He'll show up when life seems so dim
If He isn't true nothing will be lost
No paying it's free, absolutely no cost

What am I speaking of, what will you gain
It is like smelling the flowers or feeling the rain
A Spiritual touch of God, your eyes now seeing
Living in Him, oh His Spirit now is your being

Relationship between You two, now One
Spiritual sense ever growing and it's fun
But for now I need not say much more
He'll live in your heart, your very core

If you think it's a game, what is your score

Needs

When I was young my needs were many and more
Want to taste all I saw, eat the apple to the core
Older I am now and my needs seem to be few
Needs have changed from the flesh to spirit too

Have so little time to change as the age creeps up
Life is passing by, have to drink my sorrows cup
I know you don't want to read such a sad real tale
Please take the time have compassion in your sail

Winds will carry you true and some will be blessed
Trudging yourself to the top of the mountain crest
You will be shining bright, molded to perfection
Sad as can be this work may bring some rejection

You will grow into a man or woman in His Spirit
He will be your Lord, His Love, you will be near it
His Peace will descend the thick presence of God
His Power and Glory with you as Moses and his rod

Thanking God will become the speaking of your words
Closer than any relationship you have had or have heard
And when you are tired and your feet can't go on
You will be carried, what a honor, by His own Son

So when you are young let your needs be few
Stay where you started right on that pew
Make your life easy God with you always
You will be happy for all of your days.

Seven Days

In seven days God created heaven and earth
For on this planet, His image He would birth
On the seventh day He took a day to rest
Now of His creation He was fully blessed

Water covered the seas; were dark and deep
Spirit of God hovered over, He would keep
Earth without form and void, mist all around
Brought up land separated water from ground

Said let there be light, it covered the dark, gave sight
Divided light from darkness, called them day and night
Created all life, provided the seed, food for mans need
Sun and moon He called what a beautiful, loving deed

Every animal, from the birds in the air to fish in the sea
Keeping a wonderful balance from the grass to the tree
Blessed these creatures that they would multiply in kind
Fruit on the trees, nutrition in the ground, good and fine

God created man in His image, dominion in His birth
Made man and woman to multiply and fill the earth
Showed man what He made it was all for him
Saw it was good, rested, sanctified the day, a Gem

HARDSHIPS, ILLNESS, FIGHTING THE FIGHT

Deep Emotions Rise In Our Hearts

Seem some people and their things will not part
Building life for self with possessions from the start
From the ways of possession, truth isn't seen
And when you look in their eyes there is no gleam

Only in the moment do we seem to trust life
Nothing is sacred not even a mans wife
And to look further to the heavens, possibly a God
These paths of life most would rather not trod

Then comes tragedy in the life we made secure
Our possessions and money cannot bring a cure
These are the moments and times we look for more
Looking for truth in our heart, boundaries at the core

Find nothing in ourselves that alone will suffice
Seems like in our heart it's near as cold as ice
Boundaries and beyond, dare we travel in our need
How much will be lost, how much will we bleed

Our flesh is beginning to become a weakened state
Suddenly there is need for our friends and our mate
Even more something spiritual is forming around
Afraid to go to God for He may now only frown

For we have denied His call, His mercy, His grace
Now all our wealth and possessions seem out of place
Oh God will You help me I haven't been so good
I 'm not even sure that I've ever understood

Please accept my apology, I'll give you all I possess
Take my ugly life and please may You possibly bless
Will you accept me in to Your Kingdom and Grace
Will You save my life Jesus, I remember deaths place

Where You gave Your Life for all who would believe
Come into my heart, oh Lord never leave
Show me how to live and become whole
Save me oh Lord, save my soul

Divorce

This one is one of the hardest to bear
Put our whole life into another ones care
Then to see them drift away so fast
Thinking this love would forever last

The time is terrible for one, more it seems
For one is leaving, one has lost their dreams
Then is there are children how do we tell
To explain this tragedy, life just did fail

Must give love, it's been ripped from you
Taken away oh dear God what can I do
They will see love when going to your ex
When they come home what to do next

Empty in your heart only One that can fill
Marriage in God was our heart, His seal
Remember God does forgive, must move on
Will move forth and will rely on His Son

Do the best, the very best you can now
Ask Jesus for help, He'll show you how
To go on with life with a new mate or not
Just remember by His blood you were bought

Find some friends that understand the same
With them you will find there is no more blame
New love or not His love is with you
Jesus your first love will always love true

Father Where Are You

Father oh Father where are you this day
We down here on earth are looking for a way
To live a life worth while, with You in our eye
We want You to help, while we try and we try

We haven't seen Your movement for all mans needs
A long time now, world unraveling in its deeds
War and hatred is gaining its strength now
We need to come together, please show us how

You walked and talked with man in the beginning
It seemed like mankind was going to be winning
Then sin pounced upon us and death became clear
No longer did You walk with us, no longer near

Many years went by man always flirting with sin
You came and destroyed, man couldn't win
Finally, You sent Your Son to show us Your ways
He was sinless and pure for all of His days

Once again You walked with us, many didn't see
Instead, they beat You and hung You on a tree
This time You tricked him, took sin to the grave
The devil was beaten, deaths keys he then gave

You freed all the dead, in prisons they were held
They rose to the Father and behind left they hell
You came back and showed that You still did live
You freed us from sin, this gift You freely did give

So now the world needs You again they do suffer
The devil is everywhere there seems to be no buffer
Come down again and show us Your power
We need You so much knowing not the time or hour

Oh God come to all, and speak in our ears
Give us Your love in the place of our fears
Call out now oh Jesus, Savior of us all
We pray and we listen, we wait on Your call

Fight With The Armor Of God

We war not against flesh and blood
But against spiritualities in high places
The flesh wars against the spirit
The spirit wars against the flesh

Our weapons are not carnal but spiritual
For the taking down of strongholds
So what is our armor and how
Must be in a spiritual style

Helmet of salvation to protect our head
Breastplate of righteousness guards our heart
Sword of the Spirit Gods Word, Jesus
The belt of truth, He is the truth and the light

Feet, they are covered to carry the gospel of peace
Shield of faith to quench fiery darts from the evil one
Praying always with all prayer and request in His Spirit
Being watchful to the end with your trust in Him

Not by power or by might but by my Spirit says the Lord
Vengeance in mine saith the Lord God Almighty
Submit to God, to resist the evil one, tell him to leave
Be filled with His Spirit, pick up the cross daily

Live in Him, for Him, with Him in His plan
If you do this you will have taken a good stand
Stand on the Rock, the Rock of our Salvation
Relationship with Him you'll experience elation

Gods Direction

To have Gods direction and to stay in His path
This is the best that it gets here, life on this planet
Holy Spirit is the One who gives us our direction
If we let Him, He'll take our life, put a plan in it

He'll live in us; we will be One with Jesus, and Father
Speaking in our ear until we say we want no more
Then He is gracious and will leave us alone
We will then feel empty from deep in our core

There is nothing worst than that oh so empty feeling
Like when we lose a love one or have a divorce
For one it is sorrow, for the other not as crushed
For one goes to heaven, one has another course

So where are you my friend, where do you stand
Are you to love God and love not one another
I say not, for if you do, the Bible says you are a liar
Suddenly not around all our sisters and brothers

Change now, repent, stop bringing down Gods church
Many are watching Christians when we live in a sin
Little ones too, are you thinking they don't see you
How can you do this to your very own kin

Repent now my friend; show Jesus your heart
Turn around from old ways and let Him lead
Don't be a fool and destroy family and friends
Feel a tear for your sake, for Jesus did bleed

I Pledge

I Pledge allegiance to Father God and His
only begotten Son
To one nation under God and Jesus Christ they're One
To the Flag of America and the republic for which it stands
I believe in freedom of religion for every woman and man

I believe in God as most men do and hope
we can have peace
I am not concerned if another man prays on
a corner or does cease
As long as we don't fight and choose that
the other is wrong
Then we may even be able to someday together sing a song

Religious wars seem to never end so lets not let one start
If we don't judge one another then we will
be doing our part
So if one man wants to pray to Jesus it is all right with me
And if another one wants to pray to Allah then let it be

Let us have liberty and justice for all, there's only one God
Unless you think a miracle team created earth and its sod
It all goes back to Abraham and from there to the first man
We can all believe in what we want and
live together we can

A majority runs this country and every man can vote
We must let the majority alone; don't call
the minority a joke
Until the numbers say that there is more
of one than another
Let us just look to each other, on this earth being
sister and brother

The difference between church and state we
worried about, was from before
Like in England and Rome when the State
ruled the church, and more
There way was wrong and it proved itself so
and we fought to be free
Leave it alone unless there are more of you
and just let each other be

The majority will rule out you few if you fight
this fight too soon my friend
The laws will through time put you down the
majority will soon defend
Let Justice take its place in the time and way that is right
Why don't you one or two just stop and end this fight

I want to state one more thing as I put this thought to rest
I've tried nearly all religions, spiritually I did quest
I finally met Jesus, after many years religion
became real to me
Too much education takes you away from Spirituality,
blinded, can't see

I Seek You Lord

Lord I've done all that I know to do
I need Your help I'm in a real mess
Seems I've tried to follow all of Your ways
Depending on You my God all of my days

You told me in scripture help is at hand
Troubles come like the number of the sand
The devil himself causes enough on his own
The world around, to You their not prone

Many religions and trouble within the flock
Against each other, bombs ticking like a clock
Clicks abounding little Love to go around
Everywhere it's happening in cities and towns

Killing and blaming pointing fingers at each other
Kids living alone they haven't even a mother
Father is gone too, he went his own way
He thinks life is about how much he can play

Starving children, divorce all the things that You hate
To some that live on earth it seems that You are too late
You must show us now in a way that only You can
How we can Love, share, and show man Your plan

It has to be You to lead the way to go now
That You come back now or show us exactly how
To live in Your Love to receive Your power too
That we can continue on, it has to be of You

You are the Creator, few of us that know You
Thinking that Your way on earth would grow
Come back to us Lord, You are our first Love
Holy Spirit, land on us now like a white soft dove

Let the latter rain fall for all of mankind here
Holy Spirit it's You that we need to be near
Miracles and wonders from heaven above
Let it be in Your Love, Love, and Love

Lady With A Hard Life

A lady once had a hard road to live
She felt like all she ever did was give
Wanted to receive more day by day
In Gods way she began to pray

Things little by little did change, oh yes
Little things began showing their best
She saw His plans came slowly but true
And began not to be so down and blue

But the best was to come, not yet seen
His promises were good, she began to lean
She slipped and fell into His arms so strong
Thank You Lord, You were here all along

So she sat down and gave it all to her Jesus
She's now knowing He wants to please us
So He poured out a blessing big as can be
Changed her life as she gazed at the tree

Then came her miracles, one and another too
All she dreamed of, His Grace came through
Life now changed, her family and her plans
Thank You Lord, You did it all, as only You can

My Life Or Yours

My life is changing with age
The wrinkles are ever so deep
Plastic surgery is a true rage
But even that doesn't keep

Youth passed by so very quickly
Some lived more than others
Then some just had to be sickly
Some die young like my brother

Suffering is none to hard for some
Hardly a day of pain in their life
Others cry out all day, come help, come
Happiness is thin, little left but strife

Then some cry out with pain in their heart
Seems it is as hard as suffering can be
Sadness in their life from the very start
So very hard to smile and be happy

If you see one that is suffering or in pain
Please be gentle as you can to them
It might help them to have hope and be sane
The little you did might shine like a gem

Have you anything that you could offer
Could you bow before God for this man
Might you learn that life is never for sure
Give a helping hand, in your heart you can

Shut Down The Tower

Time of the Tower of Babel, God stopped man
Stopped the building and changed the language
Communication ahead of its time would start high tech
Would make us like Him, we would make earth a wreck

Time and inventions were as slow as a worm
Planted; sowed first the seed than the harvest
Man had much time to think of Gods ways
Moral values still were sad most of the days

Abraham asked to give his firstborn son he so loved
Told by God his seed would bring many as the sand
Yet he had to follow and carry out what God did ask
Sacrifice prepared by God allowed son to live, he gasp

God brought His own Son into the world
Gave His own life, sacrifice for all of mankind
Man could now be with God, a better way and place
Jesus taught many good ways, He was full of Grace

Now communication returned in a powerful way
Communication worldwide, bringing much power
Coming to know how God does some of creation
Weapons and war need more Godly relation

Seems like the world, coming to hate as the devil
Wars and more wars with hate abounding about
No peace left for most living this beautiful day
Technology can be used making a good place to stay

So maybe its time to shut down the tower again
Spiritual revival we are looking to see, all nations
Religious wars, all believe that You are theirs too
One world, One God, come Lord Jesus in truth

Son Of God

Jesus You came and gave a wonderful sacrifice
You gave Your life on Calvary it was not nice
You gave Your life that we could be with You
Opened a door to heaven this I believe to be true

In these times many do not believe You are Gods Son
We tell them the story of what has been done
That You gave Your life freely, it was not easy at all
So we all could live, You took sin into deaths call

So many religions so many that are taught now
Many doctrines about You many people do bow
We can't bring many to You without Your Holy Spirit
Please help us to speak and help people to hear it

Bring Your presence to stand with and touch
The people we pray for they need You so much
Give them what You give us, a knowing You are real
Show Yourself to them and help them kneel and feel

The reality of God, that Your Son is Jesus
Holy Spirit too and that Your here to lead us
Then more will bow down to God and His Son
For You dear Jesus they will stop and not run

You are the Son of God; Jesus
Show Yourself my savior
Bring our love ones into Your Spirit
Give us Your Word and help them to hear it

You Jesus are the Son of God

Many Nations Sorrow

Being the leader doesn't make one able to lead
Knowing mans sorrows, yet not filling the need
Fresh and salt water can't come from the same mouth
Doesn't matter if you convince the north and the south

The plain truth is all the people want to hear
Don't want the politics, can't survive in the fear
Just want bread and butter on the table each night
Oh leaders do you really have God in your sight

There are many needs in food, shelter, and trust
The rich man that wanted to follow Jesus, a must
Couldn't live both lifes, its one or the other to prevail
Having much is ok, living for and loving it, we fail

Who is wishy washy, who is coming to the table tonight
Am not thinking that one is all wrong or the other all right
All is not wrong, all is not truth, and loving
money can bring evil
It can eat you up like the crops are by the boll weevil

Destruction and sorrow have you two thought it through
You talk of the middle class and the poor people too
Remember if you're feeding the rich and
ignoring the poor soul
Can you look to your own heart and imagine the end toll

With so much to offer, not holding back some parts
You say you care for all the people, then please start
Seeking God Almighty with all heart and soul,
will find Him
Embrace Him, He's holding His hand to you,
fill your cup to the brim

Young Soldiers

Lord I see all the young soldiers go fight in the war today
They haven't even known what becoming
a man is truly like
That is the USA and the way of life in the land
they were born
Some go to fight and possible lose their life, still ride a bike

Then there are some who give their life in a battle of glory
Sadness hits us all at home regardless of race
or political beliefs
Yet their life is gone they come home in a
body bag so young
In all I can think or do, there somehow doesn't
seem to be relief

Father God I pray that You would save them
before their fall
They wouldn't just be a number in the death
toll that we count
But in everlasting life, Your mercy would
give them redemption
That You oh God will take them up, up to Your very mount

The other deaths we don't hear about much, civilians too
Oh God, we trust you would consider them in
Your call that day
As some were not taught or even brought up
to know You Jesus
For their soul Lord God my Savior, Messiah,
my friend, I pray

Consider my prayer and all those who read
pray with me too
Father God please send Your Holy Spirit
to everyone involved
So all on earth have the chance to know You,
hear Your voice
Oh God, we all live, and stand in You, let them be called

MIRACLES AND PRAYER

Easing Problems

Try not to create more problems than you're dealt
For life is somewhat difficult, its very best day
If you can make peace with another then do it
What goes around comes around, it might stay

If married your mate needs some good time too
Surely each can do something nice for the other
For your kindness in giving will come back to you
Are you loving and kind to your sister and brother

Now if you are single you don't have to be a loner
Your kindness can go out many ways to another
Sharing a smile to someone, whether sober or stoner
You would have done to you, if you were the other

What am I saying in writing verse, am I clear
Exalt another higher than yourself my friend
Help a man or woman a stranger or one dear
When doing so the Spirit of God you will send

For His last command was to love one another
He said this is a new commandment for all
For all who believe, every sister and brother
In doing you may help another to hear His call

Emergency Prayer

A loved one in emergency, emotions are deep
Into our hearts the fear of losing them does creep
Some will try anything to keep them from dying
All the while feeling like they can't stop crying

Then comes the moment only a miracle will do
Maybe God will help now, need to pray through
Call all friends and ask them to pray as well
Lord grant a miracle, to Your glory we will tell

Must stand on faith don't let doubt creep in
Oh God please help, and forgive us our sin
My dear friend Jesus, You went to the cross
Pray to the Father it's hard to bear the loss

You know Lord we will love you either way
This person deserves help, for a while to stay
We pray together for Your touch to come near
Say the word to heal, Your salvation will be clear

I cry from my heart that You will do this for me
Let all that are involved know Your love and see
You still do miracles on earth this time and day
I ask You Father, in Jesus name I do pray

Father I Need Your Help

Father, I have some medical problems and I need Your help
Father, in Jesus name I really can say to You
I need Your help
Father, creator of heaven and earth I ask You for Your help
Father, the great I Am, the One who is All in
All I need Your help

Jesus, can You pray to the Father and ask Him
to help me now
Jesus, You are our intercessor and I send my faith
for Your help
Jesus, You are my savior and best friend as well,
will You help
Jesus, it's by Your strips and pains that scripture
states I am healed

Holy Spirit You are God indeed and You are
here with me now
Holy Spirit You are my miracle for it is by
Your Spirit I am healed
Holy Spirit I listen for Your still small voice
that I may get my direction
Holy Spirit speak to me now that I may have
a true healing for I need You

Father You, Holy Spirit, and You Jesus are
One and I live in You
Jesus You said You live in the Father and He
in You and I live in You
Holy Spirit You are the Spirit within me and
by Your power heal me
Father, Son, Spirit, Holy Trinity speak the word
and I shall be healed

Father let me praise and lift Your name for the touch
you bestow upon me
Father in the name of Your son Jesus by Your Spirit
let my body be healed
Father send Your Holy Spirit that He will have
it in His heart to heal me
Father Jesus is my friend, Savior, and fulfills
all my needs in You

Jesus I reach for Your garment, as did the woman
with the issue of blood
I have faith that You oh Lord will touch me for
Your glory and Gods Glory
Let the people hear my testimony of Your great
Love and healing in my life
Let my life be spent testifying of You Father God,
Holy Spirit, Jesus

Heal me from this moment on, oh Lord I
receive Your healing touch
Heal me now Lord I believe in You as the great
healer of all time
Heal me now Father in the name of Jesus that
You may be glorified
Now glorify Yourself by Your Spirit, oh Lord
I receive Your healing

Handshake

There was a day when a handshake was binding
A mans word stood strong, he would not renege
An oral agreement truly about the same thing
When someone had need, help he would bring

He went to church took his whole family along
He gave of his time for the good of another
To honor the Lord, in hard work he believed
A man in hard time he would try to relieve

A widow or family in need found food at the door
They knew it wasn't just because they were poor
It was Gods Grace and the commandment to Love
The crop came in, at the door was more from above

Each did his sharing and it came back to him
In his families health or good buys at the pen
God is a man of His Word, sharing His best gift
Came to earth, the form of a man forgiving all sin

He gave His own life for all mankind
Took mans sin, took man out of his bind
Killed, died and buried and rose from the dead
Holy Spirit teaches us to do all that Jesus said

Trusting You, like the handshake with a man
Joining in unity, praying together, making a stand
Loving one another, with Your help we can
Pour Your Spirit upon us, holding our hand

Jesus Possible Prayer

Father I pray with heavy heart
That the time will soon start
I know I will be the sacrifice
Once in for all, I need advice

For fear nearly comes upon me
As I look at the future to be
Give me strength and Your thought
For by my blood, mankind will be bought

It's distressing to think, I am about to see
Sins suffering coming so fast upon me
My Father in heaven come and fellowship
Before I have to face this Holy hardship

In the garden now I call, the hour is upon me
No one can help me on this earth, only Thee
Must I drink this strong cup, as to take my life
Sin past, present and future will cut me as a knife

Not my will but Yours alone, I give my life for man
I will do, my love is true, and the only one is I that can
Lay mans sin upon me now I am ready to die to sin
Every sin now and future and every sin that's been

My victory is complete, resurrected, all now done
Please share my victory, all of my daughters and sons
I'll be with you in the days to come in all of your lives
Together we shall be one day, I so love you my wife

Living Miracle Still

Told by many doctors I was to die
Then specialist told me the same
Then a third looked me in the eye
Said make my arrangements, end game

My two boys about nine and ten years old
Mother had left I was to raise them alone
Arms weak and numb, surgery I was told
Liver is gone, on transplant list, the virus is bold

Lord what will happen to my children I asked
Why am I the only one willing and able to love
To care for and give my life to them, no task
Way I can is You give a miracle from above

God help me, been through so much
Praying for years for help from above
Know what I need is Your healing touch
Send it from heaven like You did the dove

Said to the doctors, I will not die
Prayed on my knees and face each day
By day I did love and by night I did cry
Please oh God will You allow me to stay

Then came His touch I knew He was true
Told all I knew He was moving in me
I will no longer be sad nor will I be blue
Here today seven years past, God is the key

Miracles For Gods Glory

Miracles are done for glory to God
They can be for anyone that lives
A new convert can get one too
He can give one to a person like you

Supernatural power does it you see
Now Jesus is the resurrection power
For He raised from the grave to live
Came to His disciples to share and give

The miracle that is done is for His glory
Man can't make one happen no matter his story
Yet man living in His Spirit, walking in His light
Well He may do one through him, Gods might

Miracles can happen driving down the street
Can happen if you pray to God in the feat
So never give up be at peace with Him
Please don't think your chances are slim

Let go and let God, true saying indeed
Should be a believing mans creed
Pray for healing if His presence is clear
If nothing else let His love cover your fear

Sharing God

I wish I could tell you what I've learned for myself
For all of my life I've learned this one secret
By earnestly going to God and trusting in Him
I never seem to fail when the winnings are slim

For in those times of hardship and pain
When there's no way out that I can figure
No one to help, seems they've all gone away
Even my dog seems like he's some kind of stray

I don't seem to fit in any ones time and space
They all hustle around trying to get some gain
They also turn the corner to hardship and pain
The crops are dying but there is not a drop of rain

Have you ever been in these sorts of encounters
Do you feel like you are standing alone
Are you wishing for some kind of miracle
But you really don't want to be hypocritical

If I could only be there to tell you what I have learned
Yet I don't want to enter your space when you're down
For it looks like I'm trying to sell this Jesus I know
Like cramming down your throat how can this grow

Just tell me that I can be of some help in your life
Let me know that you're all alone and in need
I promise what I tell you is from my heart for real
This secret that I have has an everlasting seal

Singing In The Rain

We've heard it said of a formal and a latter rain
And look forward to the latter, in a world that's insane
We want to see Gods Spirit poured out on man
Who can deliver this, only You God can

The world is in distress and confusion like never before
We have much knowledge and high tech at our door
Our conveniences are many in America for sure
But for all the killing and hard hearts, we have no cure

Wars are abundant; people are starving to death now
People are suffering, stopping it, we don't know how
We talk about Jesus being the answer and way
To us He is, but to many He is very far away

So how can we get God to move for us this day
We can't do a thing so we just talk and pray
Some put forth some effort, and save one or two
But how much does God move for me and you

For only He can bring forth this wonderful day
Where mankind can really see Him work the clay
To heal a person of a illness or much pain
This in His mercy would bring much gain

Let us sing in the rain for such a day to come
Let us pray on our face till our knees are numb
Let us cry out to Him to come and help us now
He can show us the way and the only true how

Come Lord; pour out Your Holy Spirit on man
We worship and sing to You to complete Your plan
You can direct our ways and show us power and gain
And we will all just be happy and sing in the rain

Show Us All

Are we to think our minds will continue as they are
Are we to think we might be soaring like a star
Can we know what it is to be in Gods own hand
Do we have a way to make our last earthly stand

Will we change from our body to a spirit existence
How far from our reality, how far is the distance
Will we still see and know what our loved ones here do
How far will the separation be from our family, so blue

Will they know we are around, or in the hand of God
They can't see anything but a corpse in its final nod
So final and forever does death look to our eyes
There is so much sorrow and grief, oh my the cries

Now if we believe in Jesus there is not so much pain
Yet with all the worlds' ways, who are really the sane
Is it the one who believes in Jesus or another way yet
Is there any one way that is a solid and sure bet

If you believe this or not it's up to you right now
I have seen and had many a miracle to show me how
To believe in Jesus was the name that was said
Lived and did not die on thin ice I did tread

Oh if You dear God would come back and show us
For there is many a way the people of earth do trust
Pour out Your Spirit that we can all truly see
Let us all see You so we for eternity will be

All with You, don't want to lose a relative or friend
You Father, Your Son Jesus, the Way You did send
So let us all see You in Your Glory on this planet
And let our salvation together be cast in granite

Under Her Wings

The Eagle is beautiful in its flight so smooth
She swoons through the air like a high glider
Landing in her nest to feed her needing young
Beautiful songs about her are loved and sung

When her babies are ready they must learn to fly
So under her wings she nestles them so close
Into the air she glides with them in her mind
Soon they will be dropped doesn't seem kind

They try and they fly little wings getting tired
So far to go till they have a safe place to land
Weakening now their muscles are giving out
They begin to call out to mom, they do shout

Mom sweeps down under her wings they go
Safe now they are feeling happy as can be
Back to the nest and all turns out so well
Gods' love can be seen in this story to tell

Now when we are weak our Lord is so strong
He'll take His children under His wing as well
He will protect His children as the eagle did too
A good example of how His love comes through

Walking In Jesus

I haven't very much money
Yet, I have Jesus in my heart
Seeking the land of milk and honey
And in His Spirit we'll never part

Difficult life, troubles galore
Happiness and sorrow blending as one
Looking to the Father seeking much more
Co heirs with Jesus, His begotten son

Peace within, in the midst of pain
Physical declining, death at the door
Knowing of miracles so much to gain
Praying for others, the sick and the poor

Caring for others, His truth within
Parting from life's sinful ways
Only in His death am I free from sin
Desiring now to live with Him all my days

Suddenly healing, resurrection touching me
Dealing with life's problems, one by one
Faith and humbleness now real to see
Having been touched by Jesus His Son

He restored my life and abundantly
Now people all around can see
His Word is true, He is Lord
All completed for you and me at Calvary

We Worship You Lord Jesus

We worship You Jesus with all our heart
With our mind and strength we worship You
We sing songs to You Jesus from the days start
You sacrificed for us and we know it's true

You're worthy of worship and songs galore
You have made a way for us to have fullness of joy
You're worthy of praise when we walk out the door
You opened the way for every girl and boy

We have a life with You as Your friends
We live in Your Spirit, in our soul, in our heart
We leave behind, traditions and trends
No matter our condition we have a new start

Give our teachers Your wisdom to teach
Give our workers Your strength to bear it
Give our preachers Your Spirit to preach
Give into our life the desire share it

Now let us be the body of Christ
Use us as Your own to show Your way
Double anointing, anoint us twice
We'll show in our life, You're here to stay

Holy Spirit come upon us as we worship in truth
Use us as Your own to show Your true way
Let us praise You Jesus in all that we do
And in Your Holy Sprit is where we will stay

We worship You Jesus, we worship You

Wonderful Gifts Of The Spirit From God

Jesus has the Gifts and with the saints He shares
You may have many or few He distributes and cares
All of them come from the same Spirit with Love
The very same God that works them all from above

Gifts are given to man, His Church for profit to all
We the Body of Christ, One Body, move at His call
To lift up the Church we are strong in singing and praise
Fall into His Spirit to move in the gifts all of our days

Wisdom to one, word of knowledge as well,
some faith for all
Gifts of healing, working of miracles too and
prophecy a call
Discerning of spirits can help to see who we can
trust and is true
Tongues and interpretation of tongues gifts as well,
the last two

In total trust and life in His Spirit, Love the Lord
with all your heart
Love your neighbor as yourself, be forgiving,
don't judge, a good start
In our relationship with God let us share our gifts,
for His Body He gave
For His Power and His Glory in His presence,
His gifts, the way He'll pave

Your Eyes

Your soul emerges to me
I could just look and stare
The beauty that is there

When your eyes look at me
There is power in your look
Awesome glory is their role
I feel them entering my soul

When we look at each other
Intercepting each ones being
Seeing deep into each soul
Love is our only goal

When I see God in your depth
What we see no one can tell
Looking deep into your being
Our eyes are not just seeing

Now to make this understandable
To let you know what you can do
You are all this capable too
Your can see each other true

ABOUT THE AUTHOR

I was born in Cincinnati Ohio in 1946. My family moved to Tucson Arizona in 1947 and I grew up in Tucson. I went to College for two and a half years, then moved to California and worked for a paper company for over ten years. I returned to Tucson because a stepson had asthma and we were told he needed to be in a dry climate. He had had a respiratory arrest so we made the move. I then went to a private college that specialized in medical careers and graduated in Respiratory Therapy. I worked for many years in healthcare and have done everything from Emergency Room, to helicopter transport, to working on a open-heart surgery team. The last ten years of work were in a home health company.

I have two sons Thurston and Roman and one daughter, Debbie. I raised two more daughters that are as my own, Heidi and April. I am happily married to my wife Mary who is a blessing from God, and I love her deeply. I have two-step children Maja and Erik. I am very happy and have a wonderful relationship with my children. I am thankful to the Lord for He alone has granted me joy through much tribulation. This book is dedicated to Jesus.

Now let me share some of my trials that led me into my

current walk with God. About ten years ago the hepatitis-c virus had taken its twenty-year toll and my liver was scarred with cirrhosis. I just had my forth surgery, this time major neck surgery repairing three disc with plugs from my hip. I was caring for my two sons and my liver was giving me major weakness and fatigue. I knew I was getting weaker and decided to move with my sons to Nebraska to get to know my three grandchildren. I also wanted to give my boys a better education and life in a small town environment. I was now disabled and needed help as well. My daughter was willing to help and another daughter had decided to move to Nebraska with us as well. I bought a nice little house with my Social Security lump sum and was on my way to learning of a closer relationship with God. In a small town environment it is much easier to become closer to God than I had ever experienced before. It was like moving back to the fifties.

Seven years ago in Nebraska I became critically ill with end stage cirrhosis. I had my gall bladder taken out at which time they did a third biopsy on my liver and I was given six months to a year to live. The lab and gastrointestinal doctor confirmed this and my regular doctor said about a year or possibly two. I then went to another gastrointestinal doctor in Omaha about 160 miles from home. This specialist told me there was nothing that could be done besides a transplant and I needed one soon. He also told me my health might not be strong enough for surgery. The Lord came on me and my faith skyrocketed, I found myself telling the doctor and all his staff I was going to live, that God was with me and I proceeded to give a sermon about Jesus. They all looked sad then started to feel the presence of the power in my words and started smiling and getting positive with me. I was preaching! Went into the waiting room where everyone was looking down feeling like they were at their last stop, kind of felt like a funeral home. They all started getting happy and I told them that they were all right whether here or with the Lord. They clapped. I never let go of God again and the healing began. I had several years where I was so sick and weak that I didn't know if the next morning would come or not. I was given test after test, put on heart medication after they found a blockage and on and on. I was still caring for my boys that were now sixteen and seventeen and needed Gods help. What I'm leading up to is that through many nights on my knees and face before God I have survived it all. I am off heart medication, after being on them for six years, ulcers healed, hemorrhoids healed, hepatitis-c has gone to a crawl and my liver is getting better.

So after being told seven years ago to make arrangements for my funeral, I am now holding my own and know I have had many miracles and healings to get this far. I brought the boys back to Tucson with me as I felt I needed to be closer to a major hospital and there may be some new treatment that and I wouldn't be able to do it 160 miles away from Omaha. My physicians know there is something different about me and can't explain it. I have one doctor that is Christian who believes I have had a miracle with my liver. I had over 15 blood results off since 1983. This is the first time since I was 33 I have normal blood work except for one thing and it is almost normal. I have been this way for near two years. These poems are a direct result of many days and nights of prayer to live. I had to raise my two sons for the last 11 years alone. I needed to live for them and cried out for their sakes. The Lord responded and one-day things began to turn, first the turning was in me and the way I believed, the way I lived, the way I stood on scripture and the way the Lord directed me. I wrote a poem when I had a huge turn around in my health about two years ago called Getting A Miracle. I was asked to write a short analysis of my healing for church and tried and tried and finally the Lord just put this poem in my spirit and it was written through His Spirit in five minutes. I had written poetry most of my life, but this book is about Jesus and the things I have learned and prayed for, with Him always being the answer. He is truly my all in all and I give all credit and glory to Him for the healing that is still progressing. I know I would not be here without His move, His touch, His Spiritual leading. He is the light of my life so this book is called Getting A Miracle—Light Covering Darkness.

D. J. Shrewsbury